ANNE MARIE MCALEESE is from Portstewart, County Derry, and has presented the award-winning *Your Place and Mine* programme on BBC Radio Ulster since 1991. Before meeting Dot Blakely just over twenty years ago, Anne Marie knew that birds flew and that there were a lot of them. Since then, with Dot's expert guidance, she has become an enthusiastic birding student. Dot's regular slot on *Your Place and Mine* is a favourite with listeners: Dot supplies the bird knowledge; Anne Marie peppers their conversations with fascinating facts about the places they visit.

DOT BLAKELY was born in Bangor, County Down, and it was as a young girl, on walks with her dad in the grounds of Bangor Castle, that her fascination with birds began. She is a member, and former committee member, of the RSPB NI; an ornithologist for the Woodland Trust; a member of the Wildfowl & Wetlands Trust; the founder of Castle Espie Bird Watching Club, and of North Down Bird Watching Club which she still runs; and an official bird counter and surveyor for the UK Wetland Bird Survey. For the last thirty years, she has shared her extensive knowledge with eager birders and novices alike through her classes, walks and talks via Belfast Metropolitan College and Queen's University Belfast, and through her hugely popular appearances on BBC Radio Ulster's *Your Place and Mine.*

GU00356910

For Peter —
(with sincere thanks!)

HOMEBIRDS

Anne Marie McAleese
& Dot Blakely

Happy Birdwatching!

Anne Marie McAleese

·THE·
BLACK
·STAFF·
PRESS

First published in 2022 by Blackstaff Press
an imprint of Colourpoint Creative Ltd
Colourpoint House
Jubilee Business Park
21 Jubilee Road
Newtownards BT23 4YH

With the assistance of the Arts Council of Northern Ireland

LOTTERY FUNDED

Printed by GPS Colour Graphics Ltd, Belfast

A CIP catalogue for this book is available from the British Library

ISBN 978-1-78073-340-1

www.blackstaffpress.com

To the incredible people that I have been fortunate to meet on my journeys across the country over many years, particularly Dot, for her enduring patience, good humour and cups of tea. And to the amazing places in Northern Ireland that I've visited, especially Portstewart, my home town, and Portrush, where I first came to appreciate seagulls, who are very definitely your birds and mine.

Anne Marie McAleese

This book is for the birds; for my husband, Terry, who has had to listen to me chittering on about birds for years, and for my family; and for my birdie friends. Home should always be where the birds are.

Dot Blakely

Song

In spring, their music fills the trees and hedgerows with
blossoming life and song before the rippling green appears.

Throughout the long summer days, they are a welcoming call
to the rising morning light and the gentle benediction of a
country dusk.

Autumn finds fewer voices but their songs are sweeter in the
slow golden air of changing days and falling light.

In the still and silent days of winter, they are a welcome gift,
bringing tiny dashes of colour and light into the short,
dreich days.

Throughout my year, they soar and flutter around me like
the very notes of the music they carry within. They are my
morning gift and my evening benison.

Anne McMaster

Contents

Foreword

For over three decades I have tuned into BBC Radio Ulster on a Saturday morning to the dulcet tones of Anne Marie McAleese. Her programme, *Your Place and Mine*, brings us on a voyage of discovery each week as she explores the people, places and stories that make Northern Ireland unique.

Each place she visits has a story to tell or reveals something about our built or natural heritage. It was the latter that first brought Anne Marie's co-author, Dot Blakely, to my attention. Dot has devoted a lifetime to sharing her love of birds with anyone willing to listen and, together, she and Anne Marie are the perfect combination when it comes to encouraging people to get out and about to learn more about the beauty and importance of our feathered friends.

Having travelled the highways, byways and indeed many laneways together to search out myriad birdlife over the years, it feels inevitable that they should have written a book. In *Homebirds*, Anne Marie and Dot share their stories from across the whole of Northern Ireland, complementing them with stunning photographs that will assist the reader – whether professional or amateur birdwatcher – in identifying birds in their own back gardens.

Patrick Cregg MBE
Ambassador, The Woodland Trust

The first person I ever saw with a bird eating from their hand was Anne Marie McAleese. It was in a short video made to promote her BBC Radio Ulster show, *Your Place And Mine*. The only other time I have seen such a thing was when Snow White's hand was the perch, though I suspect the Walt Disney special effects department may have faked that one.

Over the next seven years, during my time as the producer of *Your Place and Mine*, I learned more about Anne Marie and her birdwatching friend, Dot Blakely. I also learned about the wide variety of birds that we have in this part of the world and how they live their lives – like the pair of swans who set up home at a caravan site at Bushmills. Dot and Anne Marie followed the progress of the swan family over one calendar year, reporting on the birth of their cygnets and on how the swans nurtured and trained them until they were ready to make their own way in the world. It was as enthralling as a family saga.

Anne Marie and Dot are so gifted in telling us about birds. As this book shows, they make us realise why we should definitely take time to look up at these wonderful beings; to see and hear just who we share this world with.

MICHAEL BRADLEY (AKA 'THE UNDERTONE')
PRODUCER, BBC NORTHERN IRELAND

Introduction

My first real bird memory is of going with my dad to see the seagulls flocking around Lansdowne and Ramore Head in Portrush. I was pretty young – probably smaller than the seagulls – but my enthusiasm for these wonderful birds stayed with me.

It was not until I met Dot, however, that I really became interested in birds. She was brought in as a guest on *Your Place and Mine* about twenty years ago, and from the start, her appreciation and understanding of nature and birds shone through. I found her passion and enthusiasm infectious. She took me her under her expert wing and tried hard to impart some of her extensive knowledge. She demonstrated how to hand-feed the birds, how to identify them by sight and sound, and provided incredible insights into how birds think and why they behave as they do. I was her willing, albeit challenging, student.

The two of us met regularly to explore Northern Ireland; to see just what awaited us on our own doorstep. Because that's the real secret of birdwatching: the beauty of birds often goes hand in hand with the beauty of the place where they make their home. Birds lead to trees; to rivers, lakes and streams; to forests and woodlands, mountains and hills; to country and coastal landscapes, urban and rural environments. Birdwatching also opens up the whole world of butterflies and moths, wildlife and insects, wildflowers and hedgerows, fields and meadows.

There is much to be gained from an appreciation of the natural world and there are no more natural stars of it than the birds who were here long before we arrived and will be here long after we have gone. Their inbuilt communication system should be the envy of NASA: morning, noon and night, in an impressive array of *calls*, *scrakes, tweets, twits, coos, chirps, chits, chacks, teeks, ticks* and *tacks,* they conduct their business efficiently and with gusto.

It remains something of a phenomenon that each year, at precisely the same time, thousands of birds throughout the world instinctively leave their homeplaces and fly thousands of miles without the aid of any navigation tools to sunnier climes where the living is easier.

They exhibit a range of dazzling courtship displays, and are immensely talented singers. When the work day is done, or about to begin, they can charm the bird that takes their fancy out of the trees and into their wings. Their warbling and calling prowess is nothing short of awesome. And size doesn't matter in the least. From the diminutive goldcrest to the wondrous golden eagle, their chanting, crooning and serenading can travel across fields and along rivers, and reach the highest mountain peaks, echoing through dense forests and parks, instilling delight and wonder in equal measure. Their feathery coats, in an eclectic range of colours, are accompanied by a remarkable assortment of variously sized beaks, legs and crests, ensuring that they are always dressed for the occasion, whatever the setting may be.

To see a kingfisher dive at great speed, to watch a gannet plunge into the depths of the sea or a heron nonchalantly pounce and successfully catch a made-to-measure fish is a thrilling experience. Such skills are, no doubt, the envy of many a fisherman the world over. Birds are also talented trapeze artists and can balance perfectly on electricity cables for as long as they feel the need, content in the knowledge that they will not slide, slip or fall.

Watching these creatures and witnessing their acrobatic feats first-hand has been a revelation and has brought me deep contentment. Wise beyond their feathers, birds embody the notion that there is great joy, serenity and pleasure in simply existing, and in existing simply; food, shelter and company are the staples for which they live and die. Our lives can only be enriched by an appreciation and understanding of nature and birds. Had I not met Dot, I might never have become fully aware of this wonderful fact. That I feel even slightly more knowledgeable about these inspirational beings is in no small measure down to her ever-accommodating mentoring.

It is a matter of great personal satisfaction for Dot when her friends, family or students undergo a Road to Damascus conversion. The 'eureka moment', as she calls it, comes when they least expect it and the 'bird lady' takes a moment to savour the joy that has been successfully passed on.

That notion of sharing knowledge and joy is at the heart of *Homebirds*. Ironically, Dot and I first discussed the possibility of a book during the Covid pandemic, at a time when we couldn't meet up and do any actual birdwatching together. But if the lockdowns taught us anything it was that we need to take the time to enjoy and appreciate nature, and most especially birds, more than ever. As time wore on and we became accustomed to the unfamiliar stillness that enveloped the world, it seemed that our feathered friends were way ahead of us. The new silence in the air allowed them to be heard, seen and acknowledged like never before … and they were in particularly perky form.

Dot and I are not, by any means, technical wizards, but we kept in touch by email, we talked over video chat, and we relived all the wonderful birdwatching moments of our friendship. The result is this book, which we hope provides helpful, cheerful advice and guidance about birds and places across Northern Ireland.

Our shared hope for each copy of *Homebirds* is that it will become well-thumbed and slightly battered-looking through regular use. Take it with you on days out or sit down with it in advance when you're planning an adventure. Flick through the chapters to decide where you want to go and take a note of the types of birds that you're sure to see. Use the great photographs generously provided by fellow birders as a reminder of what to look for when you are on site. We'd be delighted if, in time, your copy started to sport traces of routine handling, such as tea or coffee stains, raindrops or even bird poo.

As this anonymous poet once put it:

Have you leant upon a gate, without a need for words,
to take in nature's wonder, and to listen to the birds?
Yes, leaning on a gate is a thing we ought to do,
it helps us to unwind, and such moments are so few.

Seeing a particular bird for the first time is an unforgettable feeling and we'd love to think that you too will be inspired by the natural wonders you witness. There are real and measurable benefits to our physical and mental health from being outside; the great outdoors is there for the taking. The trick is to realise this and experience it.

ANNE MARIE McALEESE

It's been more than three decades since I began to take birdwatching more seriously. In that time I have changed not only as a birder but as a person too. I get great satisfaction from helping people understand our amazing birds and the ecosystem in the same no-frills way that I acquired the knowledge.

It was during a childhood trip to Bangor Castle with my dad that my interest in birds was first sparked. We'd been walking around the castle grounds when he pointed out a robin's nest in a nearby tree trunk and told me never to look into the nest or disturb a nesting bird. His advice stuck with me.

When my own family grew up, I became more aware of our outdoor spaces – the woodlands, parks, fields, rivers, sea and coastline – and, of course, the birds. On days out to Scrabo Tower with my friend Daphne, we would watch the wonderful nesting peregrine falcons and kestrels, and my childhood love of birds was quickly reawakened. The more we travelled to different places, the more

I really began to take notice of the beautiful countryside that we are blessed with right across Ulster.

Before long, I decided that I wanted to do more; to somehow be involved in the lives of birds in a meaningful, useful way. The Wildfowl & Wetlands Trust at Castle Espie seemed like a natural fit. It was on my doorstep and word had it that they were always glad of volunteers. I have offered my services there for over twenty years and, in that time, also started up the Castle Espie Bird Watching Club (now the North Down Bird Watching Club, based at Crawfordsburn Country Park, Bangor). I am a member of the RSPB and also served on the committee for seven years. I'm a bona fide bird counter and surveyor as well, and rarely leave home without my trusty clicker.

I'm lucky in that I connect easily with nature and bird life. I think of the birds as my friends, and they never fail to impress me. They are supreme weather forecasters: they can travel over land and sea without a map; they can catch a fish by plunging into the oceans; they can build a home without plans and line it with an ingenious range of natural, foraged items to create warmth and comfort. Without them, I would have no reason to get up at three in the morning in springtime to go to a woodland and listen to the dawn chorus, the most beautiful music in the world. Or in the winter, to battle against hail, rain, sleet and snow as I try to count hundreds of waders and brent geese before they fly away … or my fingers fall off.

But birdwatching is not just about these amazing creatures, it's about the entire ecosystem, and this is what I try to pass on to anyone who wants to learn. Whether it's people who sign up to my birdwatching classes or those who attend the talks I give to different clubs and groups as part of my role as ornithologist for the Woodland Trust, there is nothing better than introducing adults and youngsters to the wonderful birdlife that can be found in our woodlands or along our shores.

I've been fortunate in that I have been able to pass on my knowledge to the general public: I've had a regular spot on *Your*

Place and Mine on BBC Radio Ulster for over twenty years and often contribute to other programmes across the BBC network. I've even been on television from time to time.

From the first day I worked with Anne Marie, it was clear that she would be a dedicated student and a great teacher herself. She was eager to learn about the birds we encountered, and I was keen to find out more about the places we visited. Over the years, we have explored a great variety of landscapes, and found many, sometimes elusive, birds, and while we often managed to get lost, frozen, soaked or sunburned along the way, it has never put us off. We both know that there will be plenty of rewarding birdwatching days ahead.

We sincerely hope that this book will help ensure the same for you and will give you renewed respect and appreciation for the marvels of nature that we are lucky to have on our own doorstep. After all, as I'm fond of telling Anne Marie, the more you look, the more you see.

Dot Blakely

How to Get Started

Whether in the garden, backyard, balcony or in parks and woodlands and along coastlines, birds are the heartbeat of the seasons and, like the sky, they are everywhere. The language of these living creatures is universal and it's easier than you think to become fluent in it. So, if you are thinking of braving the elements to do a spot of birdwatching, here are our top tips for getting started.

Where should I go?

To begin with, talk to your friends, family and neighbours: What birds have they seen locally? Can they recommend any good birding spots or vantage points? You may also want to look out for classes in your area or take a course.

But really, it's as simple as just going outside to have a good look and listen. It's best to think of somewhere local that's handy to get to. Parks with lakes and seats are ideal. While you're there, watch what you can and savour every moment. If there is a lake or pond, there will usually be ducks – so what can you see? Is the bird in the water? Is it like a duck but not a duck? Has it a green-coloured head and neck with a white line at the bottom, a grey back and silvery wings? Keep notes and when you get home, look it up; you'll enjoy the satisfaction of confirming that what you have observed is indeed a mallard duck.

Once you find your personal birdwatching place, it's a good idea to go back to exactly the same spot, watch even more closely, find what you saw the last time and then, armed with more confidence, really observe the colours of the birds, the way they feed and how they interact. By this point, you are very probably a confirmed twitcher.

Things will now rapidly begin to fall into place.

With each new bird you see, try to note the size and colour. Compare your findings to another bird you might know and soon, another breed will be added to the growing list of ones that you recognise instantly. With practice and dedication, your identification skills will develop quite quickly and your ears will become more attuned to the songs of different birds. Before you know it, people will be firing quizzical looks in your direction as you tiptoe in circles around a tree, neck strained, scanning the trunk for bird poo.

Dot and I are now oblivious to the bemused passers-by and if we do happen to notice them, we're inclined to think they don't know what they're missing.

When's the best time of year to begin?

Birdwatching is seasonal, so there will always be something different to see. A good time to start observing is around March, in the run-up to spring. This is the onset of the singing season: our avian minstrels will be joined in gardens, woodlands and parks by distant relatives from Southern Europe and Africa, such as chiffchaff, willow warbler and whitethroat, who come here to breed. They also appreciate the climate: sunshine and rain combine to create an ideal green environment bursting with insects, more than enough to go round the recently relocated flying army.

By the end of June, most of the new arrivals, cheek by jowl with the locals, will be busy raising their families. Things go very quiet. As the singing stops, the teaching begins. The young must learn quickly what to eat and where to find it, where to shelter and how to avoid trouble. Parents move around woodlands, gardens, and other habitats contact calling, making it harder to see the birds. In the birdwatching world, this is break time.

By September it's all go again as the visitors and their young return to warmer climes. Autumn is a spectacular time of year that both novice and advanced birders relish. Thousands of wildfowl and waders swoop in after a long journey from Arctic Canada and Northern Europe to overwinter in the seas around the coastline and in our rivers and lakes. The sight and sound of mass numbers of brent geese flying overhead is unforgettable. They are drawn inexorably to the gourmet food – the grasses, invertebrates, and crustaceans on offer in the mudflats and shorelines.

The wildfowl and waders stay until the end of March, and having had their winter holidays, and kitted out in shiny new flight feathers, they take to the air again, making the long journey home to breed.

By then, though, it's only a few weeks until the dawn choruses begin again. Just enough time for birders to check in on their preferred forests, parks and woodland sites, not to mention spruce up their garden bird feeders.

What will I need?

It's crucial to be aware of the weather, and in our climate it's easy to get cold or wet in the blink of an eye. Good rain jackets and trousers, a hat and gloves and walking boots for rough and unexpected terrain are worthwhile investments.

While binoculars are by no means mandatory, if you already have a pair, bring them with you and take time to practise and learn to get the most out of this handy piece of kit. Field glasses can range in size, scale and price. Like reading glasses, it's best to take advice from the experts, and your new-found fellow birders, before investing in a pair that suits your needs and budget.

Telescopes are not necessary for parks and gardens and are mostly used in winter to help pinpoint birds on shorelands, loughs and far out at sea. Optical instruments can be weighty and cumbersome, so chats with other birders can be helpful to establish what their experience has been and what will fit your requirements.

When you are out and come across an unfamiliar bird, it can

be a good idea to snap a quick photo for later study, so you may want to bring your phone, or a notebook and pen to write or draw a description. This will help trigger your memory for the research bit back at home.

There are some excellent reference books on birdwatching that can help with your research. Dot's favourites are *RSPB Handbook of British Birds* by Peter Holden and Richard Gregory and *The Birds of Ireland: A Field Guide* by Jim Wilson and Mark Carmody. You could also try to identify your bird on the internet, or with a bird identification app. The RSPB has an incredible bird identifier on its website.

But probably the only essentials you'll really need are a snack to keep you going and a flask of tea, coffee or a hot drink.

Now all you have to do is watch.

SPRING

Cygnets at Ballyness Caravan Park
© *Albert Boyle*

Greylag goose © Chris Henry

Jack and Gulls
in Ballycastle

There is no better feeling than being outdoors watching birds and nature. It is a joy and a pleasure to observe nature in this way and never fails to brighten my day.

TERRY GOLDSMITH

Despite the fact that in Irish *Baile an Chaistil* literally means 'town of the castle', there may well be an argument for renaming Ballycastle 'town of the seagulls'. For obvious reasons, it's a place they adore. Naturally, there is the lure of the sea, where they are most at home, and not quite so naturally, the appeal of a good fish supper. Between the breaking waves of the North Atlantic Ocean and award-winning catch-of-the-day eating houses, this County Antrim seaside town on the most north-eastern coastal tip of the country has a lot to offer these clever creatures.

On many visits as a youngster, I shared the enthusiasm that the gulls have for this beguiling place, especially for the tasty treats wrapped in newspaper, always best eaten there and then at a picnic table or, on a wet day, in the car, looking across the sound to Rathlin. Ballycastle is a place I return to often, savouring those delicious childhood memories and doffing my cap towards the seagulls as they patrol the harbour area, ready to swoop on unsuspecting visitors eating their fish and chips al fresco.

Dot thinks the gulls are greedy scavengers with no manners and not much going for them. Setting their considerable appetites aside,

I could watch them swoop and soar, duck and dive, squawk and screech all day. To me, they are majestic masters of the coastal breezes with a suit of clothes to match. They are perfectly designed, with yellow, webbed feet that are ideal for slippery rocks; snowy white or grey feathers, often with black markings on the head or wings; and robust, chunky bills. For my money, Lady Dot doth protest too much. But I'll keep working on her.

The whole area around Ballycastle and the Glens is steeped in myths and legends that have been handed down over centuries. Magic, curses, spells and charms are staples in the stories that the locals delight in recounting to visitors. Supernatural beings like the grogoch, the banshee, the pooka, leprechauns and sheeries are leading characters that no self-respecting glensman or woman would dare to question.

From the heartbreak of Deirdre of the Sorrows to Robert the Bruce hiding in a cave on Rathlin Island, the sorcery of Aoife turning the Children of Lir into swans and the tragedy associated with the naming of Fair Head, Ballycastle has the power to cast its own particular spell.

Legend has it that Fair Head was named after a beautiful, fair-haired girl who lived in a castle on Rathlin Island. She had many suitors, and in a fight between two of them, one was mortally wounded. As he lay dying, he whispered to his servant to dance with the maiden on the cliffs below the castle. The servant obeyed and they danced nearer and nearer to the edge of the cliff until eventually they tumbled to their deaths. From then on, the place on the shoreline where the young woman's body was washed up has been known as Fair Head.

It was not, however, these kinds of bewitching charms that attracted landowner Hugh Boyd to Ballycastle in the eighteenth century. Instead, he saw in it an opportunity to create one of Ireland's earliest industrial towns. A man of vision, he developed the Ballycastle Colliery Saltworks, built one of the first tramways in the country in the town, along with a new harbour and linen and glass works.

Coal was also extracted locally and, along with wine bottles, leather, soap and linen, was exported to America, England and also distributed to a burgeoning domestic market. The beach in the town is about a mile long and stretches from the marina to Pan's Rock. This area is part of the Ballycastle Coalfield Area of Special Scientific Interest (ASSI), which is cited as having the best exposure of a coalfield sequence in Ireland, containing important evidence of this early industrial activity.

I've arranged to meet Dot at the car park near the ferry terminal. It's a cold, crisp, bright day and the sun is dazzling and dancing to its own tune on the calm, bluey-green sea. Dot has been chauffeur-driven today by Terry who loves cars and Dot. Their friends Richard and Val have come for the run too and when I arrive, the picnic is already under way. One of Dot's mottos is 'never leave home without a flask' and, as I feel the same way about homemade egg and onion sandwiches, we are a picnic match made in heaven.

As the only picnickers in the car park, Dot is slightly concerned about the opportunistic gulls. She needn't be. A friendly jackdaw,

Jackdaw © Alan Gallagher

that we'll call Jack for the purposes of this story, puts them well and truly in the shadows. This is Jack's territory and it turns out that he's well known in these parts. The locals are very fond of him and feed him every day. It seems that he is enamoured with them too, displaying none of the outward signs of shyness or trepidation of his cousins, the rook family from a few miles up the road at Loughareema, also known as the Vanishing Lake. Without a care in the world, Jack hops around making his presence felt in front of his small, but appreciative, audience.

In my mind, Dot is a bird whisperer, a Doctor Doolittle-type character that the birds know and trust instinctively. She talks to them, chirps with them and sings along with them. So it's no real surprise, but still a magical moment, when Jack flutters on to Dot's shoulder and is in no rush to leave. She and Jack chat away about bird things and when they have put the birding world to rights, Jack performs a final flourish, landing squarely on Richard's head, as if taking a bow before the curtain comes down on his last performance of the day. Richard's theory is that the cocky bird has a sweet tooth, adding quickly that he has picked the wrong picnickers and has no chance.

Since we are here anyway and in the company of so many of these iconic coastal birds, Dot gives in and we talk seagulls. She says that at some stage in life, many of us will have at least heard, if not seen, these imposing, mostly white birds, with black and white wing tips. There are only five species of gulls here in Northern Ireland, so once you get your eye in, they're straightforward enough to identify.

© Alan Gallagher

At only 36cm, our smallest gull is the **black-headed gull**. Its head is actually more brown than black and it sports a red bill to match its red legs. In winter the head changes colour and becomes white with a small black spot on the side. The red legs make them relatively easy to spot and this particular species has more nesting colonies inland than any other gull found near farmlands.

Lesser black-backed gull
© Chris Henry

Herring gull © Juliet Fleming

The **lesser black-backed gull** is 53cm to 55cm in height and the **herring gull** is next in line, at 55cm to 66cm high. These two gulls are very similar, both white with black wing tips and a heavy yellow bill with a red spot. The herring gull is a tough, hardy bird that takes no nonsense. The lesser gull has yellow legs and white upper parts, while the herring wears pink stockings with light grey upper parts. Both very stylish. The clue to differentiating these two gulls is in the name – the lesser black is exactly that, with wings that are more dark grey than black. The herring gull wing is a much paler grey, similar in colour to a herring fish.

© Juliet Fleming

The **common gull** measures up to 40cm. The face is softer and snowy white, though in winter this changes to a grey-brown colour. Its beak has a streaky yellow-green hue, perfectly colour coordinated with its legs. Despite its name, there are fewer common gulls than black-headed ones but they share similar coastal territory.

© Stephen Maxwell

The biggest gull of all – Dot calls it 'the big beast' – is the **greater black-backed gull**, at between 64cm and 79cm. He's the head buck cat gull and no other gull would dare cross him or pick on him – quite the reverse. They have been known to throw their considerable weight around and are rarely out-manoeuvred in a fight.

Dot says they have cross-looking, sharp faces, giving the impression that they've been in a bad mood for a very long time. Their bills are heavy-looking, yellow with a red spot, and they have pink legs. In flight they resemble a caped crusader and with jet-black back upperparts, they are well-named. This seagull is a formidable predator, capable of swallowing an egg or gull chick whole.

Sometimes a little knowledge can be a dangerous thing. All the gull chat reminds me of what I now know is a one-legged lesser gull that stands on the roof of the house opposite my parents' home in Portstewart. We christened him Hoppy. Dot says either his other leg didn't come down properly when he was born or he was in a fight and lost. Either way, he can usually hold his own very well when it comes to feeding.

One wintry, frosty, February day, Hoppy made a detour around the corner to the road outside my house, looking very smug and delighted with what seemed to be a golf-ball-sized fatball in his beak. To my dismay, his delight was short-lived. His one leg had only just touched down on the iced tarmac when a much larger herring gull swooped in from nowhere at rapier-like speed, quickly relieving him of his prized gourmet lunch. He looked very forlorn and so, I think, did I. Better the seagull you know than the ones you don't.

Birds adapt to the environment and are great indicators of change in it. If they have trouble finding food, water, shelter, then we know we also will soon be in trouble.

CATHERINE JAMESON

Swans and Whiskey in Bushmills

*Oh, the joy of it, if you're quiet and just see. Just see.
Don't try to watch too hard. Lower your expectations
and take pleasure in the simple things. There is reward
at every turn. They're watching you too!*

Denis Chambers

There's been a bottle of unopened whiskey in my house since 2008. It's a special edition that marks the 400th anniversary of the start of the distilling of whiskey in the village of Bushmills and the beginnings of a global brand. Now sought after around the world, the whiskey is known simply as Bushmills or, closer to home, as Bush. The delights of this 'water of life' are wasted on my palate but I do savour the envious looks from visiting connoisseurs who cast a jealous eye in the direction of the beautifully-branded wooden casket that stands on top of a bookcase in my living room.

My repeated visits to Bushmills and tours of the distillery over the years have yielded many nuggets of information, ranging from the absolute certainty that the village owes its name to the River Bush and a large watermill that was built there in the early seventeenth century, to the more mythical claim that the distillery is haunted by a ghost. Either way, Bushmills is a unique place that more than merits a visit whether you like a tipple or not.

As far as international fame and world firsts are concerned,

Bushmills punches well above its weight. The Giant's Causeway is merely a giant-sized hop, skip and jump away and almost a million people a year visit this UNESCO World Heritage Site.

In January 1883, and following in the footsteps of Finn MacCool, the first section of the world's first hydro-electric tramway between Bushmills and Portrush was opened. It was a sad day indeed when, in the summer of 1949, the last tram made its final journey along the eight-mile stretch of line from Portrush to the Causeway and into oblivion.

Thankfully, further along the coast, Carrick-a-Rede Rope Bridge and Dunluce Castle are still very much intact and breathtaking in equal measure. All in all, locals and visitors alike are spoilt for choice when it comes to planning a day out in and around Bushmills.

Dot is never stumped when it comes to planning a birdwatching day out. Her latest idea is intriguing because, for my money, it sounds more like a year out than a single day. She explains that, on several visits to a caravan site on the north coast, she's been absorbed by a family of swans who live there all year round. My natural curiosity means that I'm ready to be engrossed as well.

Her directions to the location are straightforward – go past Bushmills distillery and then turn left into Ballyness. This rural caravan park opened in 2000 and is surrounded by fields, trees, hedgerows, rivers and man-made ponds. It's an oasis of calm country life that the past and present proprietors have taken care to create and maintain. It's easy to see why they are winners of a David Bellamy Gold Conservation Award: there are three wildlife ponds that are home to a pair of swans and numerous moorhens and ducks, and the woodland areas have several well-used nest boxes.

Dot was here shortly after the park opened to carry out a bird species report for the then owners, Olive and David Dunlop. They wanted to know what birds had made their homes in the park and how to increase the biodiversity in their ponds. Dot recalls that even then there was plenty of bird life around: robins, blackbirds, chaffinch,

© *Ballyness Caravan Park*

blue tits, and house and tree sparrows. The farmhouse at the time had a B&B run by Olive's aunt, and Dot stayed there for a couple of days. She smiles as she recalls that even the swallows were made welcome when, like contortionists, they swept in underneath the front door.

Dot's contacts in Ballyness have been in touch to let her know the good news that six cygnets have hatched. She is unashamedly champing at the bit to meet these tiny new arrivals, as is Terry, her chauffeur for the day and, I suspect, more often than not, the chief tea and sandwich maker.

Leaving home early, on a bright sunny morning, we make time for a quick catch up with Olive. She too is a keen birder and she brings us up to speed on the recent antics of the happy family of swans.

On the stroll towards the ponds, Dot explains that, in general, moorhens do their own thing. Mallard ducks instinctively know to stay out of the way of the swans when their young arrive and greylags are equally savvy, neither bird wanting to risk the definite possibility of being driven out or even killed by the adult swans if they feel there's a threat to the food supply. The swans' major concern at this stage in the cygnets' life is feeding them and ensuring there is as much food as possible.

It's vitally important that people respect swans and their territory, especially at this crucial bonding stage. Make no mistake, they will attack anyone or anything that comes too close. This sage advice also applies to dogs, who should be kept away or restrained on a lead.

With this in mind, we approach the large pond quietly. The sight of a fully grown swan in the wild is a thrilling experience. We are close enough to appreciate the dazzling, snowy white plumage of these graceful creatures. The two adults glide serenely past on the bigger of the two ponds, followed by six adorable, tiny, grey, feathery cygnets with their mini-me-sized black beaks.

Mum and dad are at top and tail of the morning parade, keeping a very close eye on their beautiful brood. We stand stock still on the edge of the bank as the big male makes a detour in our direction. Dot is fluent in all bird language and interprets the snort fired in our direction to mean, 'Keep your distance'.

There have been moments in Dot's birdwatching career when she has been left speechless by the behaviour of birds. What happened next in the ponds at Ballyness ranks among the most remarkable birding conduct that she has ever witnessed.

The adult male returned to his family, then paddled towards the overhanging branches of a willow tree, extended his neck to bend and then dip the branches into the water before offering the juicy leaves to the young to eat. This is highly un-swan-like practice. Swans usually feed by filtering the water to remove the food they want. Before long, the cygnets imitate their parents and begin to peck at water plants and insects on their own, and within two to three weeks they too will start to 'upend' and eat from below the water's surface.

What's happening in the ponds at Ballyness is very different. Dot's theory is that swans, and indeed many birds, have a great ability to adapt and change depending on the environment in which they find themselves. They are highly intelligent creatures, with 20/20 vision and impeccable hearing.

They are known to be loyal partners who mate for life, and there are numerous stories of swans dying of a broken heart if their partner or young are killed. Perhaps this is why swans are fabled in so many classic fairy tales and myths. My esteem for these resplendent birds is rocketing by the moment.

We continue to watch in awe and wonder, becoming acclimatised to the snorting and quiet calls of the cob (male) and pen (female). We don't want to outstay our tentative welcome – like good guests, we know when to leave to ensure a return invitation.

Towards the bottom of the pond at the other side, the mallard are feeding freely on the water weed, upending from time to time in sequence, like skilled synchronised Olympic swimmers. The chiffchaffs, here from Africa to breed, provide the musical accompaniment. Their song resembles their name, *chiff chaff, chiff chaff,* and today their backing singers are the willow warblers, demonstrating versatility and a lightness of touch by delicately nipping through the musical scale from high to low. If this was a competition, today's performers would receive full marks all round and a standing ovation.

We leave in the hope that the swans especially will treat us to many more encores in the months ahead.

No matter where we live, when we go out for a walk or even look out of our window, we see these wild creatures at first hand. No need to go to a zoo or safari park. No wonder they are universally loved by everyone.

DAPHNE JONES

Swans with their cygnets at
Ballyness Caravan Park
© Albert Boyle

What's in a Name
at Drumnaph

*When I was a teenager, there was a blackbird who
visited our garden regularly. We called him 'Jack the
Black' and his wife was christened Jill. They returned
to the garden for several years and we loved to watch
them. Blackbirds with their yellow beaks are still
a favourite. It's a moment of joy to see one in my garden.*

PAULINE CURRIE

As you come towards Maghera on the A29 from the Coleraine side, there are a couple of signs pointing towards a woodland just a few miles from the town. The first one says Drumnaph and the second one, further down the road, points towards the same place but it's Drumlamph that's written on the sign. Either way, this is a uniquely special place, the jewel in the crown of the Woodland Trust's ancient woodland sites and the result of a successful collaboration with the Carntogher Community Association.

It's also somewhere that Dot is extremely fond of. She has worked closely with the Woodland Trust for many years and shares its belief in the inestimable value of trees and their ability to enrich people's lives. The official title of this secluded green gem is Drumnaph Community Nature Reserve and the Woodland Trust owns approximately 80 acres of the land at the eastern side.

Here there is a mixture of both ancient and newly planted

woodland, as well as some wetland habitats. In the western section of Drumnaph there was once a farm owned by the O'Loughlin family, and when an opportunity arose to buy more land here, the Woodland Trust and Carntogher Community Association jumped at the chance. It is a patchwork of ecological habitats that includes ancient woodland, wild flower meadows, ancient grazing habitats and wetlands. The site is managed and continually monitored by both organisations for the enjoyment of the local community and visitors alike. Many people spend time here enjoying the tranquility that only a beautiful space like this can give. As I was about to discover, with Drumnaph, one visit is never enough.

Dot had been promising to take me here for some time but was determined that the first trip should happen in the spring or summer when everywhere was looking its best and the birds would be in fine form too. This particular day in May was the kind that makes you feel glad to be alive and that, combined with the prospect of a guided walk around this new place, added a definite spring to my step.

Dot's directions to Drumnaph were spot on and since it's less than thirty miles from where I live I wasn't overly concerned about finding the car park beside the wood, where we'd agreed to meet. That was until the mysterious signpost affair.

In truth, I passed the meeting-point more than once, confused by the signs and wondering whether there were two different Drum-somethings? Having overshot the runway for the third time, a passing walker did eventually direct me to Gortinure and then Grillagh Road. On arrival, Dot informed me that she had been watching my antics from a distance and keeping her fingers crossed that I would eventually notice her frantic waves.

Weeks later, it turned out that I may not be quite as dopey as I first thought. A man on the radio explained to me that the name Drumlamph is pronounced locally as Drumnaph, which means either 'the ridge of the elm tree' or 'the ridge of the wild garlic'. He also said that next time Dot and I were in the area we should look for

McCartney's Oak, named after a grazier from the 1860s who in the summer used to shelter under the tree's huge canopy. A good excuse for another visit.

On the day that we meet, Dot is keen to see if we can find spotted flies. Given my confusion about getting here, I don't declare that I thought we were looking for birds. As we meander along the initially grassy, then stony path, we pass picture-perfect Easter lambs and I deduce from the directions the walker gave me earlier that the stream we can hear is the River Grillagh. Without doubt, this is a haven for many birds and, Dot adds, otters, hares, dragonflies and damselflies. More flies. The plot thickens.

Dot is savouring every moment. The willow warblers are practising their musical scales diligently, over and over, up and down, up and down, while the chiffchaffs are content to sing their own name while the local blackcaps, robins, blackbirds and chaffinch harmonise.

But what about the spotted flies, I want to ask. As we approach the end of the path, it opens into a long grassy area. Dot is concentrating, looking and listening intently. Though I don't know what I'm looking for, I follow suit. My eye is drawn to a robin-sized bird, well hidden in the bushes, and I alert Dot. A quick check through the binoculars – or 'bins', as Dot likes to call them – and she confirms that this is, in fact, a spotted flycatcher.

The penny drops and Dot explains that this hard-to-find bird is much sought after by birdwatchers. These petite birds fly here from Africa for their summer holidays and to breed. They are similar in size to a great tit and Dot is doubly delighted when one flycatcher becomes two with the arrival of its partner.

It's confession time. And when I admit that I thought we were looking for a fly, Dot is highly amused. She thinks we should retire to the picnic table that we passed near the stream on the way in, where she will administer a strong cup of tea with extra sugar to try to restore my senses.

Chiffchaff © Alan Gallagher

Willow warbler © Paul Hunter

Chiffchaff (11cm) and **willow warbler** (12cm) are from the warbler family and can be hard to differentiate as they are remarkably similar. Chiffchaffs have grey, green upperparts fringed with pale yellow feathers and dark legs. Willow warblers have olive upperparts, splashes of yellow below and pale legs; they are plumper than chiffchaffs. Both birds have a dark strip under their eyes and a thin bill for feeding on insects in the trees and bushes. Chiffchaffs like to sing from high perches in the trees. Initially, their songs are the best way to distinguish between these birds. Chiffchaffs sing their own name, *chiff chaff, chiff chaff*; willow warblers go up and down the scale, from high to low, over and over again. Both birds nest close to the ground.

© Alan Gallagher

Spotted flycatcher (14cm) has strong ties with the chat family. It has a mostly grey-brown streaked crown and upperparts. The head is slightly sunken into its shoulders, which makes identification easier. The flycatcher sits upright on a low branch, usually near water or open woodland. It uses its broad bill to quickly and lethally trap flies and then returns swiftly to the same vantage point. The name 'spotted flycatcher' comes from the juveniles who have a speckled breast.

HOUSE MARTINS

Daring and darting,
Flapping, fluttering and flirting.
Swirling and swooping,
Blue-black heads with winter-white throats.
Bealtaine.

MARY MCGUIGGAN

All in a Day's Work at Victoria Park

Walking along Victoria Park in Belfast with my camera, listening to the birds singing, watching them fly from tree to tree is a great way to relax after a long day at work.

PAUL HUNTER

———

Dot is always alert and eagle-eyed when it comes to scrutinising bird life in any given place. She often holds her bird classes in Belfast's Victoria Park, which is on the way to the George Best Belfast City Airport. Despite its proximity to the city, and the fact that it's on the flight path of bigger, turbo-charged birds, this historic park is a haven for wildlife and also part of the Connswater Community Greenway that meanders along the Loop, Knock and Connswater rivers.

Opened in 1906, after the challenging task of draining the marshy land near Belfast Lough had been completed, Victoria Park was landscaped by Charles McKimm, who also built the Tropical Ravine in Belfast's Botanic Gardens. In summer, it is awash with colour from the variety of bedding plants on display and the centrepiece rose garden. The sizeable ponds attract swans, geese, ducks, herons and migrant waders.

Dot has brought her class here on a dry and bright late April morning and they are full of eager anticipation. She begins with a walk around the outer path to identify and appreciate the assembled

wildfowl, which include swans, mallard and teal. After a lunchtime cuppa, the keen birders follow their teacher across the bridge to the middle island pond, hoping to glimpse a kingfisher.

Curiously, instead of this picturesque, florid little bird in its usual spot, Dot notices an overhanging branch with lots of smaller branches just above the water, all coming from a leafy thicket. Dot deems this to be the beginning of a nest.

Her suspicions are confirmed when she notices a busy coot hard at work sorting out twigs and grasses, twisting and turning them to make complete circles. Nearby, the female is in complete control of the design and build, while the male awaits instructions on what to do next.

On receiving his commands, he slips back into the water, paddling swiftly to the far side of the pond and up and then under some long grasses. Moments later he re-emerges with a beak crammed full of nesting material – small sticks and dry, thick and thin grasses. In his haste to return to his better half, his cherished bounty begins to slip from his bill.

He keeps going regardless, his head bobbing up and down frantically in the water; the faster he paddles the more nest paraphernalia he loses. By the time he makes it back, his stash is considerably depleted, with maybe only five single reeds left. Intrigued and anxious to know what happens next, I'm already thinking that we could christen him Mr Bean.

Dot is in her stride now as she tells me this story. There ensued a major row. Dot says she could see it in the female's face. At times like this Dot wishes she really could speak the same language as our birds but she knows enough about how they communicate and life in general to understand when a telling off is taking place. At the end of a series of loud *pitts pitt*s, the female gave him a sharp peck on his head for good measure before he was quickly dispatched once again for more material for the nest.

Back across the water to the same spot exactly, he collects another lot of nesting ingredients and proceeds to do exactly the same as before, losing most of his haul on the return leg. Dot and the class watch him continue in the same vein three more times until it starts to rain. For the rest of that day, Dot wondered about this clumsy coot, hoping that the nest got built and that he didn't end up with a very sore head from nagging and pecking.

While this particular coot might have been having a bad day, the moral of the story could well be, the best nest often starts with the smallest twig. We also surmised that in the spirit of 'If at first you don't succeed, try, try and try again,' Robert the Bruce might well have applauded his efforts.

© Stephen Maxwell

Coots (38cm) are waterbirds from the rail family. The body is slate-black and they have red eyes. It's thought the expression 'bald as a coot' is a reference to the very dramatic bare skin on its forehead, called the frontal shield, which leads down to an all-white bill. They have long legs and green, oversized toes that have two or three fleshy lobes that are helpful for swimming or walking on waterweed. Males fight ferociously for territory by leaning back and using their sharp claws. Like many wading birds, coots run along the top of the water flapping their wings to get airborne. Male and female look the same and both help to rear their young. They will fight off larger species if they overstep the mark and get too close to their brood.

The landscape is constantly being changed by man building new homes, but when birds build their nests, rear their young, and leave, the landscape is unchanged and is left as it was before.

WESLEY JAMESON

Downhill All the Way

We are so lucky to have woodlands that my children can play in and enjoy the different wildflowers and butterflies. We really do need to look after this wonderful planet.

Jennifer Finley

Towards the end of the eighteenth century, one of the wealthiest men on the island of Ireland was Frederick Augustus Hervey, 4th Earl of Bristol and Bishop of Derry. He was born in 1730, the privileged fourth son of Lord Hervey and, as such, he entered the church. He was consecrated Bishop of Derry in 1768.

The historical consensus seems to be that he carried out the responsibilities of his appointment with generosity and tolerance, taking up residence in his See, unlike many other absentee clergy at the time. But the bishop was also a flamboyant, eccentric character – a dedicated traveller, insatiable art collector and fearless builder.

Shortly after his arrival in Ireland, he conceived the mansion that would become known as Downhill House. Sadly much of the impressive, Hellenic style building was destroyed by fire in 1851. It was rebuilt in the 1870s and finally fell into disrepair after the Second World War.

The bishop and his palatial creation had their share of naysayers. After a visit in the early nineteenth century, one visitor wrote, 'It is impossible not to regret the misapplication of so much treasure upon a spot where no suitable Demesne can be created … where the salt spray begins to corrode this sumptuous pile of Grecian Architecture and the imagination anticipating the distant period weeps over the splendid Ruin, a sad monument of human folly.' Some years later, Edward Wakefield said that he had, 'never seen so bad a house occupy so much ground'.

While the scale, style and design may have been controversial, the bishop's appreciation of the location is beyond reproach. Benefitting from spectacular views over Downhill Strand and Castlerock Beach, nearby Mussenden Temple, also part of the bishop's estate, perches dramatically on a 120ft clifftop, high above the Atlantic Ocean, in the beautiful surroundings of Downhill Demesne.

The temple was built in 1785 and formed part of the Earl Bishop's estate. His idea was to use it as a summer library and the architecture was inspired by the Temple of Vesta in Tivoli, near Rome. It is dedicated to the memory of Hervey's cousin, Frideswide Mussenden.

The National Trust are now the keepers of the Bishop's daring and adventurous kingdom. His legacy is undeniable and his life and times are still a rich seam of conversation over two hundred years after his death, no doubt something that would tickle his fancy.

Driving past Downhill from Castlerock towards Magilligan, a sweeping downward bend reveals the awe-inspiring seven-mile stretch of golden sand that makes Benone Strand one of the longest in Northern Ireland and a regular recipient of the European Blue Flag Award.

This view is matched by the stunning sight of two railway tunnels that form a thrilling part of this section of the Belfast to Derry railway line. Work began on this demanding enterprise in June 1846 and with the help of vast quantities of dynamite was completed some years later, between 1852 and 1853.

Proportionately, the engineering ingenuity required to achieve this far outweighed the length of the actual train line. The longest tunnel is 275m. Blasting through this amount of basalt needed 3,600lb of gunpowder and attracted a crowd of twelve thousand spectators.

It became known as the Great Blast. When the work was finished, a banquet for five hundred people was held by candlelight in the tunnel.

On a good day, it's my preferred route to the office and on the way home, a walk on the beach is hard to resist. Dot has said if we don't find fulmars on these cliffs, there's something wrong. She seems delighted at the prospect and I'm happy too, as a quick scan through my limited collection of bird books confirms that these birds are very like seagulls. Knowing how Dot feels about them, maybe the way to her heart is through their doppelgangers.

Arriving ahead of time with my dad, who loves to walk on this beach especially, as it's within sight and sound of his mother's homeplace in Magilligan, neither of us can spy out any fulmars. But then again, neither of us have binoculars and we're not entirely sure what we're looking for or where.

Enter from stage left and the beachside car park the expert, along with her wing woman and fellow birder, Daphne. Dot says the fulmars are definitely here; it's just a matter of knowing how to spot them. Her tripod and telescope, which she often brings with her, are quickly assembled, and Dot concentrates on scanning those black basalt rocks.

Dot and the tripod are tilting upwards, zooming in and out of the craggy ledges on the cliff face. Right on cue, and as if saying welcome, a nesting pair of fulmars come into view. Just like buses, you can wait a long time for one, and then two or three arrive at the same time. They're well spread out on the cliffs, with plenty of space between them, and Dot says they seem to be nesting in depressions on bare rocks or on some grass on a ledge.

Nesting starts for fulmars when they are about six years old and they lay only one egg a year. Once the chick hatches, it's fed on a diet of regurgitated fish offal, which doubles as a defence mechanism for their young to squirt at any would-be predators. Genius.

Many years ago there were coin-operated telescopes along the promenade in Portstewart. The notion was to savour in full technicolour and close up the fantastic views of the headlands and, on a good day, the Donegal hills. Try as I might, this never worked for me, and I soon gave up squandering the 10ps gleaned from my fledgling empty-lemonade-bottle-return business.

Dot, however, is intent on me being able to use her telescope to see the birds in all their glory. She knows that patience is not my strong suit, but I have faith in her faith in me and know that she is very good at giving instruction. Before long, my eureka moment comes and I have those handsome fulmars in my sights. She is delighted and loves it when a novice sees a bird up close in a telescope for the first time.

A trance-like state seems to overcome us all and between the binoculars, the telescope and our own eyes, time stops. We stand and watch these fabulous stiff-winged, grey and white birds, going about their daily chores above our heads, flying blithely back and forth, in and out of their panoramic sea-view homes.

No doubt Dot is right when she surmises that people walk up and down this beach largely unaware of what is above them. Fulmars are here all year round, mostly staying out at sea, but returning to the cliff ledges to breed and then feed their babies. Their predominant food is the fish offal that they scavenge from the fishing boats found in deep waters.

We spend an unforgettable morning watching these seabirds take off from the cliff ledges. In these moments, with narrow wings outstretched, gracefully gliding over the sea, they are masters of all they survey.

Higher up, on the same cliffs, there are nesting cormorants as well as shags, who prefer to build their homes lower down, closer to the water. Peregrine falcons nest on the higher ledges too, ever ready to catch a meal of pigeons, waders and smaller birds on the wing.

Dot, Dad and Daphne are major fans of cups of tea. Like the Martini advert from the 1970s, it really is 'anytime, anyplace, anywhere' – I am outnumbered. And who am I to argue with the three Ds.

© Paul Hunter

Fulmars (47cm) are seabirds and part of the petrel and shearwater family. They have a bulky body and thick neck with prominent tubular nostrils and are often referred to as being 'tubenosed'. If they feel under threat at a nest site, they spray stinking oil produced from their fishy stomachs. The wings are long and straight, narrow and stiff, which helps to differentiate them from seagulls when they are in flight. They have white underparts and pale grey upperparts. Although they bear a striking resemblance to seagulls, their expansive wingspan means they are more closely related to the albatross.

Connecting with nature has always been my grounding. Mindfully watching a bee busy on a flower, a swallow swooping and diving, I get transported to thoughts of awe and wonder beyond me that replenish and nourish my soul.

MARY LAPIN

A New Dawn at Portmore Lough

The dawn chorus is incredible and is where I find my joy and my solace. I adore sitting in the back garden listening to my birds and watching them in the bird bath amongst the wild flowers, under a canopy of mature trees. There are so many varieties of little songbirds who sing beautifully and provide me with no end of pleasure and inspiration.

CAROLYN DOBBIN, OPERA SINGER

Invariably, the very best things in life are free and on your own doorstep. The trick is realising this and developing the capacity to find peace and contentment as a result. When this happens it is a moment to savour.

For many years, without ever knowing it, I lived only a dozen or so miles from one special place that more than meets these criteria. George's Island Road, at Gawley's Gate in Aghalee, County Antrim, leads to Portmore Lough, the jewel in the crown of the RSPB's nature reserves in Northern Ireland.

It really is a hidden gem: hay meadows in the summer; butterflies, dragonflies, whooper swans, geese and ducks in winter; and lapwings, skylarks, pipits and warblers in the spring. It's an all-year-round haven for wildlife, with both local and migrating birds arriving from Africa in winter and dragonflies and butterflies in the summer. Nesting terns, gulls, swans, waders and sometimes even marsh harriers also gravitate towards Portmore. It's also home to a herd of Konik ponies

Portmore Lough © Michael Graham

who graze the wetland and play their part in the great biodiversity story of this unique landscape.

In Irish, Portmore Lough means 'lake of the great landing place'. In fact, it's a small lake that drains water into nearby Lough Neagh. It is roughly circular in shape and at over 700 acres punches well above its weight in terms of global significance. The lough and its shoreland is a designated Ramsar site, which means a wetland of international importance. It's also a Special Protection Area and an Area of Special Scientific Interest.

At one stage there was a castle here, built in 1664 and removed in 1761. It is also the presumed location of the Portmore ornament tree, whose demise in the windstorm of 1760 is lamented in the Irish folk song 'Bonny Portmore'.

My first visit was memorable for several reasons. The Konik ponies had just arrived from Poland. Intent on exploring this wild landscape and meeting the new tenants, I headed into the great unknown, proudly clad in my navy and pink-polka-dot wellington boots, a memorable present from pig farmer Kenny Gracey in Tandragee.

The Portmore RSPB warden at the time, Seamus Burns, was not only a very knowledgeable man but also a patient and caring one. We ploughtered through the soggy, springy wetland in search of the beautiful miniature Polish ponies, who, unsure of the strangely attired woman with microphone in hand, seemed to get further away the closer we got. The trek was hard work and at the halfway point my left boot gave up and, in a fit of pique, refused to budge from the mushy terrain underfoot, while my leg sallied forth unaware of the disconnect between boot and foot.

Sadly, a photograph of what ensued doesn't exist but the memory is indelibly etched in my mind. A slow-motion slump backwards, hand pointing forward, microphone and lead saluting the air – in seconds I was spreadeagled, imprinted in this comfortable marshy bed. Trapped. In between the laughter and my guide's panic-stricken facial expressions, we managed to uproot me and the boot and continue the quest to meet the now highly bemused ponies who had observed our shenanigans. Horses for courses, I'm sure they were saying.

With this in mind, there was more than a wry smile on my face when BBC Radio Ulster and Radio Foyle announced a collaboration with RTÉ and fifteen other European countries in a historic all-night broadcast from Portmore Lough in County Antrim on the shores of Lough Neagh.

In a broadcasting first, the idea was to present a night filled with nature and most importantly birds, from this beautiful place – home to a dazzling array of feathered creatures, horses and, for one night only, me and Dot, as presenters of this special, seven-hour, live radio programme.

The idea revolved around the dawn chorus and the activity in the run up to this early morning, springtime spectacular. International Dawn Chorus Day is always on the first Sunday in May. Naturally, the birds wake up at different times across the world. The more we thought about it, the more it seemed like a Eurovision Song Contest for birds.

Dot was concerned that because of our northern location we might be at a disadvantage because our birds wouldn't be up first and singing for BBC Radio Ulster – we desperately wanted to avoid the ignominy of *nul points*. Either way, it would be a historic night, resulting in a groundbreaking radio programme that went on to win a prestigious European Rose d'Or Award.

Outfitted appropriately for the cold night ahead, and with plentiful supplies of coffee, tea, sandwiches, buns, biscuits and crisps, we met at midnight on what was beginning to look like a very bad weather morning ahead. In between bouts of hunkering down in the recently refurbished wooden cabin at Portmore, we made several night-time forays down to the hide beside the lough.

Mother Nature likes to play tricks and she was in a particularly frivolous mood that night. Weather reports from all over the country used adjectives like 'heavy', 'teeming' and 'torrential' before the word rain. The sound on our tin roof confirmed that these proclamations were no exaggeration. Dot knew immediately what the birds would do in conditions such as these: take shelter, be quiet and go to sleep.

Feeling decidedly unshowbizzy, we resolved that the show must go on and as the night wore on, different countries and time zones started to waken up. In the United Kingdom, and in no particular order, blackbirds, wrens, blackcaps and robins are usually the first to perform in the early-morning concert.

Ever hopeful and undeterred by the deafening Portmore bird silence, in full rainproof regalia and with torches lit, Dot and I made frequent trips to the hide overlooking the lough to give on-air updates as the rain continued to lash down. Dot thought that maybe a fox might make an appearance after a night's hunting, but no such luck. Even the gulls were quiet.

All over Europe, green-field sites turned out to be much dryer and noisier as we listened to the latest sightings and birdsong. We consoled ourselves with the thought that we've never really had a great track record in the Eurovision Song Contest. Though we did have Dana that one year. And there was Bucks Fizz. And Johnny Logan. And Brotherhood of Man. We decided to stop thinking about the Eurovision Song Contest.

But all was not lost. As the morning light began to slowly punch through the black, grey night, the rain eased and low and behold a wren signalled his approval, stealing the show from a robin, unusually late to the stage in this dawn chorus. Tired and cold, but happy, we said goodbye to our international birding friends, conceded defeat and made for home.

Years later, Dot still maintains that we really won as we had a nesting swallow with us in the shelter the entire time. She is a major fan of Portmore Lough and believes it's one of the best places to see and hear the lively *chup chup* of tree sparrows as they dance around in the hedgerows there. The RSPB have installed nest boxes and feeders because their numbers have been in decline, and this has helped to create a strong colony for people to enjoy.

Behind the visitors centre, there is a breathtaking field of wild flowers, which has been grown specifically to provide food for summer birds like swallows, chiffchaffs, willow warblers and sedge warblers, who begin to arrive here from Africa and further afield to breed in March. The major attraction is the availability of food, created by a wet and sunny climate and, of course, the green spaces.

Flies, flies and more flies are what swallows feast on as they fly high and swoop down low, large gapes open, hoovering up anything in their path and collecting it at the back of their throats

Tree sparrow © Paul Hunter

to feed the young in the nest.

Bluish-black upperparts, a russet throat and white breast are complemented by long, pointed wings and a forked tail – these birds are made for speed. To watch a swallow turn and twist at the height of the hunt in a low-flight chase leaves an enduring impression. Before the cold weather sets in, ahead of their return to Africa for the winter, these birds can be seen on telegraph lines in large numbers, preening their flight feathers and chewing the fat.

Tree sparrows can be hard to find, but they too are part of the furniture at Portmore Lough. Sometimes you'll spot them in a small mixed flock with house sparrows, but usually they prefer open woodlands or countryside and, like the house sparrow, opt for and create colonies. Male and female look the same, with a chestnut crown and black spot on a dullish white cheek.

Male house sparrows have grey heads, white cheeks, a black bib, and rufous neck, while the females are on the plain side with buffy-brown overalls and glum, grey-brown underparts. Their dull colours provide protection in their habitat. Both birds often go unnoticed but Dot is a great advocate of the notion that the more you look the more you see.

Male house sparrow
© Stephen Maxwell

Female house sparrow
© Paul McCullough

NIGHT FLIGHT

Fold your tired wings,
And go to sleep,
Little bird,
And the night wind
Will carry you home
Across the dark ocean
On his strong wings.
You still have miles to go
But you can sleep now
And dream of golden shores,
And in the morning
I will listen to your
Song of praise,
Little bird,
Outside my window.

MAURICE McALEESE

The Magic of Monkstown Wood

Birding is often filled with heart-stopping moments
of calmness where the unfolding snapshots of nature
turn into encounters of meaning which stay in the
memory for a long time.

PAUL CLEMENTS, WRITER AND AUTHOR

A long, long time ago, Ireland was covered in trees – woods and forests provided 80 per cent tree cover. Over the centuries, as a result of the Ice Age, climate change and human activity, that figure was reduced at one point to less than 1 per cent. Today it stands at around 11 per cent, largely thanks to the good work of the Woodland Trust.

Patrick Cregg MBE was director of this organisation for over twenty years and on our numerous walks through many woodlands, he has outlined the policies and challenges of this dedicated environmental charity, and emphasised the immense importance of trees.

In his tenure with the Woodland Trust, Patrick oversaw the planting, protection, restoration and care of thousands of native trees in woods, forests and ancient woodlands across Northern Ireland. He remains passionate about this important part of our landscape and believes there is still much work to do if we are to avoid our former ranking as the European country with the lowest forest cover.

Dot and Patrick have much in common and have been friends for years. They both live in Bangor and love trees, birds and tea. They spar and banter with each other like two comedians vying to deliver the funniest punchline. So when Dot says we need to go to

Monkstown Wood, I suspect that she and Patrick have been there many times and that it's a Woodland Trust site.

It turns out that this twenty-two-acre wood was once seven big farming fields that were owned by the Housing Executive, who in 1999 leased it to the Woodland Trust for a period of 999 years. The fields were used for grazing stock until 2000, when the Trust began planting them with eight thousand trees over a four-year period.

Monkstown Wood is a quirky, calm, green sanctuary in a bustling urban suburb and sits between the Nortel site on the Doagh Road and the Monkstown housing estate in Newtownabbey. Designated a local nature reserve in 2007, Monkstown Wood has undergone a facelift, with improved pathways and waymarkers. There are four lifelike oak sculptures looming large along the course of the Three Mile Water. Throughout the year, otters can be seen sweeping though the river on the hunt for fish and small birds. There's a small car park at the top of the this woodland walk, just off Monkstown Road.

Spring and summer are ideal for a visit. Today Dot hopes we will catch sight of the dippers that gravitate towards the fast-flowing water here. It's a fair walk to get to the river but the path is reasonably flat and along the way she says the woodland canopy will be full of birdsong.

We head left from the car park towards the top of the river, surrounded on either side by blended old and new habitats. Sure enough, the robins, sparrows and wrens in the hedgerows are in fine fettle on this fresh spring morning, glad to be alive and well and living in this gratifying fusion of grassland and mature and newly planted woodland.

Even though the leaves haven't come fully on to the trees in the new woodland yet, song thrush and mistle thrush are tunefully signalling their approval of this habitat. In springtime, it's also home to chiffchaff, willow warblers, blackcaps, bullfinches and chaffinches who opt for the older hedgerows and long grasses, keeping company with butterflies and burnet moths.

The Bleach Green railway viaducts, close to Monkstown Wood
© Michael Graham

Monkstown Wood is an enchanting, wild place, and as the railway bridges come into view I know that what's coming next won't be a train, it will be Dot instructing me to look for poo on the rocks. This is a tried and tested way to catch sight and sound of various birds in their chosen territory.

Eyes fixed firmly on the rocks, I'm scanning back and forth for the telltale white markings. I'm not having much luck but, before long, Dot spies a dipper bobbing up and down on a stone in the river, before landing in the shallow river to do what he does best: dip. Not in the least bit bothered by our presence, he surfaces, having caught a tiny nymph and speedily flies past us.

A grey wagtail also wings its way under the bridge, and after some forensic scrutiny of the old railway brickwork, Tracker Blakely announces that she has found his nesting site. Like the cat that got the cream, Dot is pleased with a job well done and that she has introduced me to a new spot where I can sharpen my, perhaps slightly improving, bird-recognition credentials.

The path back takes us past the edge of the nineteenth-century woodland and old hedgerows, where house sparrows, long-tailed tits, blue tits, great tits and coal tits appear to be having a meeting of the clans, with a special guest appearance by an effervescent, singing goldcrest. A day without birds is like a day without tea for Dot. Secure in the knowledge that her work here for today is complete, we reach for the flasks and a folktale.

According to tradition, in the fifth century, Fergus Mór, King of the Gaelic kingdom of Dál Riata left his home in north Antrim to colonise Argyll and Kintyre, uniting Scotland and Ireland. It is often said he is the founder of Scotland. He died while on his way back to visit his lands in Ireland, and the story goes that he is buried at Monkstown.

Dot matches this tale with one of her own that is true. Monkstown Wood is one of more than fifty places across the United Kingdom where you can dedicate trees, benches or even larger areas of woodland, to mark a special occasion or celebrate the life of a loved one with a unique and lasting tribute. There and then, I decide to arrange a down payment on a bench for Dot. Now I just need to work out what it should say about her. 'A Way with the Birds' seems appropriate.

My wife feeds our garden blackbirds on green grapes in the summer. They love them and wait for her at the back door every morning.

GEORGE GORDON

© Chris Henry

Goldcrests (9cm) are the UK's smallest birds. As the name suggests, the male has a yellow or gold crest. Gold gives him heightened visibility as he raises the crest in a display to the female. The upperparts are dull green, with pale wingbars and two black spots that can be mistaken for eyes from a distance. With a tiny, pointed bill, goldcrests are skilled practitioners in the art of flying high while upside down. This is a busy little bird, always on the go, flitting from branch to branch, continually hungry for food and searching for flies, spiders or insects' eggs. Its song resembles a high-pitched, tiny bell and ends in twitter notes that can grate on the human ear.

© Alan Gallagher

Dippers (18cm) have a thin bill and white feathers on their upper eyelids, which they flash in courtship or as a threat display. They are chunky, with dark upperparts, a white throat and breast, a chestnut belly and short wings and tail. They will always be found around streams, sitting on boulders, bobbing up and down. Dippers walk underwater, in shallow or fast-flowing streams to feed on nymphs, insects, tadpoles and water bugs. To enable them to move freely underwater, they are covered in a silvery film of air, which traps small air bubbles on the surface of their plumage, allowing them to breathe. They nest under bridges, or in crevices on the riverbank.

Some Collective Nouns for Birds

A merl of blackbirds

A belling of bullfinch

A mural of buntings

A wake of buzzards

A run of chickens

A confusion of chiffchaff

A chattering of choughs

A commotion of coots

A swim of cormorants

A spiral of creepers

A murder of crows

An asylum of cuckoos

A curfew of curlews

A dole of doves

A puddling of ducks

A fling of dunlins

An aerie of eagles

A heronry of egrets

A quilt of eiders

A tower of falcons

A trembling of finches

A swatting of flycatchers

A gannetry of gannets

A gaggle of geese

A prayer of godwits

A charm of goldfinch

A glare of goshawks

A water dance of grebes

A drumming of grouse

A bazaar of guillemots

A screech of gulls

A posse of herons

A train of jackdaws

A scold of jays

A hover of kestrels

A crown of kingfishers

A tangle of knots

A deceit of lapwings

An ascension of larks

A parcel of linnets

A mischief of magpies

A sord of mallards

A circlage of martins

A cast of merlins

A plump of moorhens

A watch of nightingales

A wisdom of owls

A parcel of oystercatchers

A cadge of peregrines

A dropping of pigeons

A knob of pintails

A wing of plovers

A circus of puffins

A conspiracy of ravens

A strop of razorbills

A gallup of redpolls

A crowd of redwings

A worm of robins

A parliament of rooks

A grain of sanderlings

A squabble of seagulls

An improbability of shearwaters

A dopping of sheldrakes

An exultation of skylarks

A whisp of snipe

An academy of sparrowhawks

A quarrel of sparrows

A murmuration of starlings

A kettle of swallows

A lamentation of swans

A flock of swifts

A spring of teal

A committee of terns

A hermitage of thrushes

A banditry of tits

A volery of wagtails

A confusion of warblers

A sharming of water rails

A museum of waxwings

A shaft of wheatears

A fling of whimbrels

A fall of woodcocks

A descent of woodpeckers

A chime of wrens

Belfast Waterworks © Dot Blakely

Wildfowl at the Waterworks

A moment of sheer delight walking with a friend; a tiny
wren returning to its nest with a beakload of grubs,
hidden in the ivy in a tree right beside us. We were
captivated sharing that moment together; such pleasure
in the small things of life.

Dorothy Smith

The nineteenth century was a time of rapid growth in Belfast. In 1800, a Paving Board was formed, charged with paving the streets of the town. A decade later, the Belfast Academical Institution was built and in 1815 work began on the first major hospital in Belfast in Frederick Street, followed by the construction of St George's Church in 1816.

The Queen's Bridge was erected in 1843 and St Malachy's Church on Alfred Street a year later, in 1844. Queen's University was founded the year after, followed by the Harbour Commissioners Office in 1854 and The Custom House and Sinclair Seamen's Church in 1857. The Ulster Hall was built in 1862 and the Albert Memorial Clock first chimed in 1869. Belfast became a city in 1888.

Belfast Castle, Belfast Central Library, the Grand Opera House, St George's Market, the Ulster Museum and Botanic Gardens all came into existence in this industrious century.

Despite these developments, and in some cases because of them, living conditions in Belfast in the first half of the nineteenth century were less than hygienic. Squalid streets and houses that were dangerously overcrowded led to an outbreak of typhus in 1847, which was then followed by a cholera epidemic in the city during which over one thousand people died.

Perhaps with sanitation in mind, the Belfast Waterworks were established in the early 1840s by the Water Commissioner in an area of land near the Antrim Road. For two decades, the site supplied water to the city's factories and residents before demand began to outstrip supply. In 1897, a public meeting was held to decide the future of the Waterworks and a suggestion was made that the site might be used for water-based activities.

The site's owners, the Water Board, were initially hesitant, as their operation licence only extended to providing the city with water, and they were reluctant to sell the land to the Belfast Corporation. They changed their minds in 1889 when an Act of Parliament granted the Water Board permission to use the Waterworks for leisure purposes, with the condition that they didn't spend more than £500 a year on the site.

Tom Boyce, a boating contractor who operated the Ormeau ferry across the River Lagan, was duly asked to provide twelve rowing boats. Public bathing and diving were also allowed. Swimming galas and speedboat racing began in 1929, and model yacht sailing started in 1933.

Belfast Corporation bought the Waterworks in 1956 and, concerned for safety, decided to partially fill in both of the site's reservoirs. The upper pond was stocked with trout for the local angling club and two islands were built to encourage waterfowl to breed.

And it worked. The Waterworks is now very much a go-to place for wildfowl. On any given day, greylag geese, mute swans, mallards, tufted ducks, coots, pochards, goldeneyes, cormorants and great crested grebes can be found at the park. Thrushes are regulars too and enjoy feeding on the lush green grass.

There is also a community garden, where volunteers grow their own fruit and vegetables. With two children's playgrounds, good

walking paths and a sports facility, it's a vibrant, busy place. In recognition of this excellent use of an open space, the Waterworks has received the prestigious Green Flag Award a number of times.

If Dot could hand out awards she'd also give one to the Waterworks. It's an all-year-round birdwatching treat. She usually finds a parking space in or around Brookvale Avenue on the Antrim Road side, though you can also come in from the Cavehill Road. Birders and locals refer to the bigger pond as Swan Lake.

We stop first at what Dot calls the 'bottom lake' from where she can check in on the swans, greylags and gulls that congregate in this corner, ready to greet the locals and make short work of titbits that come their way. An added bonus with big open spaces like this is that they offer good opportunities to develop bird identification skills and to follow the various stages in the life of a mute swan particularly, depending on the time of year. At the Waterworks, there can be over thirty swans at any one time. Numbers like this increase the likelihood of fights between the adults.

Adult swans have a full white plumage and a thick, strong, curved neck with an orange bill. The males have a large black knob above their beaks. In the breeding season, the cob will defend his territory by folding his long neck into his back, raising his wings and surging though the water in an act of bravado that sends a clear message to any would-be intruders. The best way to work out the age of a swan is to look carefully at the colouring. Dot says the younger the swan, the greyer it is. If it's almost fully white with a pinkish bill, it's likely to be around two years old.

There's a hill in the park that leads to an overflow stream and Dot has seen dippers here, sitting on a stone in the water before hastily flying into the tunnel. Grey wagtails also fly low along the surface of the water in this area. She's also spied a nice circular area with comfy-looking seats, perfect for a packed lunch later.

The trees here attract mistle thrush and blackbirds. Greylag geese also seem very content in this well-used space and dander about or sit on the grass with their young. Dot appreciates that this wouldn't happen if they didn't feel safe and acknowledges the thoughtful walkers who keep their dogs on the lead.

Mallard and tufted ducks mingle happily with black-headed and herring gulls and the islands at the top lake attract a multitude of

Greylag geese © Paul Hunter

species that include cormorants, herons, teal, gadwall, shovelers, moorhens, coot, and little grebes. Kingfishers have been seen here too, and in the hedgerows, sparrows, wrens and robins can often be heard.

In the corner of the lake, there's a great nesting area with willow grasses and reeds growing in the water, making it ideal for willow warblers and chiffchaff. The fishermen have a cosy shed nearby and over a cup of tea, when they're not teaching local youngsters how to fish, have told Dot about the otters here and the importance of this site for a variety of wildlife.

Little did the Water Commissioner know almost two centuries ago how indispensable the Waterworks site would become to the citizens and birdlife of Belfast, and in ways that have less to do with the provision of water and more with enhancing the quality of their outdoor everyday lives.

The swan regularly accompanies me on my walk around the Broadmeadow; elegantly moving along the water's edge, its curved neck and pure white feathers are a beauty all of its own.

CATHERINE SCOTT

Fairy Tales and Waterfalls in Gortin Glen Forest Park

It is lovely to walk through Gortin Forest Park and hear the sound of birdsong and water flowing in the stream. The most beautiful sound, though, is the voices of children as they have fun in the natural environment. It brings back memories of my own childhood and of bringing my children there too. Birdsong and children's voices – the music of the forest.

SEAN HARPUR

In terms of square miles, Tyrone is the largest county in Northern Ireland. It borders Fermanagh, Armagh, Derry, Monaghan and Donegal. So it's big. After thirty years criss-crossing the highways and byways of this geographical giant, it still has the ability to fill me with awe and wonder in equal measure.

Two serendipitous encounters introduced me to this enduring place. The first one started with a conversation about feet. This unlikely beginning led to a lifelong friendship with MD, as she is known to her cronies – or Maura Devlin, 'the podiatrist', to her clients. A proud Dungannon woman, she is the epitome of old-fashioned decency and goodness. She delighted in my regular visits to her home county and on many occasions acted as an unofficial radio correspondent, tipping me off about places I should visit and people I should chat to.

My other Tyrone friend, and golfing partner, is Mr Mac. Neither of us really keep tabs on who's ahead in our golfing league table, but I'm sure that if money was involved I'd be in the red.

The main road between Omagh and Cookstown is around twenty-six miles long and it's a journey I've made umpteen times, en route to the primordial Beaghmore Stones or the An Creagán Visitors Centre at the foothills of the Sperrins or Tullyhogue, seat of the ancient High Kings of Ulster, the O'Neills. This particular part of Tyrone is steeped in history and would give *Game of Thrones* a run for its money in terms of the sheer pageantry and drama in the real lives of some of Ulster's earliest inhabitants.

In the same way that cavers experience a sense of satisfaction when they stand underground in a place where no one else has ever stood, my sense of gratification is palpable when I discover a shortcut that involves a road I've never been on before. Sometimes this happens by accident, sometimes by design, as with Strifehill Road and Old Loughry Road just outside Cookstown.

Cookstown is a busy place at the best of times, especially on market day, and an excursion along the widest main street in Ulster can take some time to complete. But not if you follow Strifehill Road and make a few left- and right-hand turns, thereby ensuring a safe and stress-free onward journey. A brief stop with a woman on the old Loughry Road armed me with this useful local knowledge, which I have applied ever since.

Dot has a soft spot for one particular part of the county. With film star looks and a fairy tale feel, Gortin Glen Forest Park is only half a dozen miles from Omagh, at the western gateway to the Sperrin mountains. My first introduction to it was thanks to Drumquin man Sean Harpur, on the occasion of its fiftieth anniversary as a forest park in 2017.

As a youngster, and on regular visits to his granny who lived in the townland of Cullion, the Gortin Glens became Sean's own personal playground. He loved traversing the slopes and valleys, hiding in the conifer woodlands and wondering what daredevil hijinks might be possible at the waterfall. As a boy he may not have taken time to appreciate the birds who were surely here then as well, but these days he certainly does, as does Dot.

She says we will find chiffchaff, willow and, with any luck, singing blackcap. It has long been my belief that Dot's unchanging sunny disposition and cheerful demeanour are a result of time spent outdoors in the company of the fascinating winged creatures she admires and respects. Scientifically, it appears to be beyond dispute that there is a direct link between good mental health and spending time in the fresh air. Forests, in particular, are cited as having calming, restorative effects on tired and busy minds. 'Green Therapy' is something that Dot has practised instinctively for many years, and is no doubt why she always looks so healthy.

Gortin forest was originally planted solely for timber production. The 1,534 hectare park was opened in 1967, the first to be established in a coniferous woodland here. These days there are five waymarked trails, all starting from the trailhead close to the main car park. They are all colour-coded and very user-friendly.

The five-mile scenic route, which you can also drive, is very popular and has several lay-bys along the way offering spectacular elevated views of the county. The International Appalachian Trail and the Ulster Way also pass through the forest. And there's the quirkily named Ladies View trail – so-called after two close-at-hand mountains, Bessy Bell and Mary Gray – which is a strenuous trek, rising to 350m. The Ladies View is a stop-off point on the five-mile route, so we're thinking that, on this occasion, four wheels might well trump four feet.

As it turns out, the wheels on both cars were sorely tested on our separate journeys to the forest. Technology can be a wonderful thing, until a sign saying 'Road Ahead Closed' throws a curveball at an easily confused satellite navigation system. This happened at Sixmilecross, a small village in the townland of Aughnaglea, half a dozen miles from Omagh. So near and yet so far.

Little did I know, as I reverted to feeling-my-way mode, that Dot was waving at me while seeking directions from Gerard and Phelim, who happened to be out for a walk near the roadworks. And little did Dot know that, inadvertently, she was phoning me whilst talking to them. The conversation is recorded for posterity and involves seeing a road down there, going right, then left, watching for the big trees and saying hello to that woman on the radio. Dot and her co-pilot Daphne successfully followed Gerard and Phelim's advice and now have a soft spot for Tyrone men.

Only five miles from Omagh and three from Gortin, we were closer than we knew and relieved to finally meet in the car park, where work was continuing on plans to reopen the Gortin Glen Forest Park cafe.

On the final leg of the journey, Dot heard, though didn't see, a cuckoo. She says birds like being close to people, but not too close. Forest car parks answer their needs very well as the trees offer a perfect escape route. Food is the big draw. Some birds will nest along the edges of the woodland, in scrub or hawthorn bushes close to any picnic tables; these also offer better access to sunlight. Willow warblers and chiffchaffs like to nest in younger, greener trees, with plenty of fresh leaves.

As we move through the older part of the forest, the trees are taller and it becomes quieter. There are high-pitched contact calls from fledglings recently out of the nest, to let the parents know where they are under the dark canopy. Goldcrests, coal tits, treecreepers, wrens and blackcaps all revel in this habitat.

At various points deeper into the forest, we hear jays screeching frantically in a bid to stave off the meddling magpies. But they are outnumbered and know that the pesky magpies will continue to harass them and any mistle thrush that show up in the nesting season. Between the rattle of the mistle thrush, the screeching of the jay and the squawk of the magpie, at times the forest's soundscape is eerie.

Dot is startled when suddenly, from nowhere, a sparrowhawk flies past at rapier-like speed, interrupting proceedings. Instantly,

Sparrowhawk
© Stephen Maxwell

the forest becomes quiet and the smaller birds hold their breath and hope they're not on his lunch menu today.

Like all forests, Gortin Glen has a large, woodland canopy that protects the inhabitants. We choose not to dally too long under this verdant bonnet, but make straight for the highest point, carefully following bends, turns and dips in the road. We go higher and higher until we reach the end of the Ladies View trail, and we three ladies feel like we could easily reach up and touch the sky.

Dot explains that at this height there now exists a totally different bird habitat that's ideal for skylark, wheatear, stonechat and cuckoo, though we don't hear or see any on this visit. She does spy a meadow pipit, which, along with buzzards and ravens, relishes circling high above the forest in the big open sky. On a better day, she has no doubt it would be a great place in which to just sit and look and listen, but today's rain has put paid to any notion that Dot's trusty fold-up chairs might make an appearance from the car boot.

From this lofty vantage point, the hardy cyclist that we overtook, battling against the rain as well as the elevation, looks like a tiny speck, dwarfed on all sides by the vast expanse of the Sperrins, Northern Ireland's largest mountain range.

On the ascent it's important to keep your eyes on the road but it's hard not to be staggered by the thrilling landscape: sika and muntjac deer roam freely; huge uprooted coniferous trees are toppled to the left by the side of the path; and this temperate, rainy day is causing steam to rise from the tarmac, which adds a ghostly dimension to the whole scene.

Before we start the descent, a man in a white van arrives. As he circles round the back to open the doors and wheels out his well-used, Gortin mud-caked mountain bike, he says simply, 'Sure, it's nice to get out.' No argument from the suitably impressed and, as yet, unmuddied ladies at the viewing point.

At times nature needs a helping hand – on the downward slopes, there are acres of thick stubble-like, two-foot high sliced tree trunks that show where the forest has been thinned out. Between Fermanagh and Omagh District Council and the Forest Service in Northern Ireland, Gortin Glen Forest Park is in very capable hands. A cherished place that will last through the ages and provide heart-stirring experiences for generations yet to come.

© Alan Gallagher

Jays (34cm) are members of the crow family. They have buff-coloured bodies, a streaked crest and a black moustache on a white chin. The distinctive blue patch on their black-and-white wings makes them easy to identify. They have a white rump and black tail. Jays collect and bury acorns for the winter. They also feed on bird eggs and have a penchant for young birds, small mammals, worms and spiders. With a raucous, scolding *scaarg, scaarg* call, the jay is heard before it is seen. Mostly a woodland bird, it flies with rounded wings, flitting from tree to tree.

Meadow pipits (14.5cm) are small brown birds, with streaked upperparts, lighter streaked underparts, a fine bill and long hind claws. Meadow pipits can be found in the countryside or in coastal fields. They will sit on top of bushes or fence posts, highly alert to what is happening

© Chris Henry

all around their territory. They have a wonderful song flight, during which the male climbs steeply to about 100 feet, after singing a series of *pheets, pheets*. The song then changes to slower, fluid notes, at which stage he parachutes down with outspread, upward pointed wings and tail, to slow the descent. The meadow pipit is a favourite songbird and usually in the top ten of the birding hit parade.

Gortin Lakes

Despite the fact that I never tire of reminding both my brothers that I am the only one of us with an O level in Maths, at the age of sixteen I knew better than to apply for a job in the bank. The advice at the time was that if you were interested in a particular sport, a financial institution was an ideal career path in terms of time off and sponsorship.

Golf aside, I was convinced that successful candidates to the bank would need much more than my passing interest in numbers. I was happy at school and content to wait a couple of years before trying out academia at the new University of Ulster in Coleraine.

My abiding memory of the three years I spent at UU is not the Communication Studies degree that I was studying but the great conversations that I had with a woman from the townland of

Erganagh, near Gortin in County Tyrone.

Mary Morgan was proud of the place that she came from and her love for it was infectious. A mature student who had moved lock, stock and barrel from Bangor to Portstewart in her mid-forties and was now studying for a degree in Education, she was a woman of substance and adept in the art of telling a good story. Her sense of place was palpable and I like to think that, by association, maybe I was learning more from her than from my lectures.

Her father, Tommy Kearney, was postmaster at Lislap Post Office on the Gortin Road. He also ran a garage business at the back of the shop and, as well as fuel, Tommy sold and fitted tyres, batteries and spark plugs. Mary's love for her homeplace, Gortin – the glens, the forest and the lakes – never wained, and long after she had moved to Bangor and then Portstewart, she continued to go back, drawn by her happy childhood memories and keen to create new ones for her own children. To this day, in any conversations about Gortin, I think of her and am thankful that I didn't fill in that application form to join the bank.

The Gortin Lakes are just as well known and memorable as the forest park. Locally, their reputation precedes them but beyond these shores, the pure artistry of these two stretches of still, deep water is, as yet, relatively unknown.

Small is indeed beautiful. At less than a kilometre long, casual walkers need have no fear – this is more of a stroll than a hike. On the way to the lakes, there's a sign for Boorin Nature Reserve, a tasty appetiser for the main course just around the next bend.

Geologists say that the modest hills that surround Boorin were created when the melting ice sheets of the last Ice Age left behind huge amounts of sand and gravel. These gentle slopes are now covered in heather, and the terrain around them is bogland. The small loughs found here are deep and known as kettle lakes.

Dot says that at the height of summer, skylarks sing here to their hearts' content, and that my old pals, the buzzards, circle lazily above them. She is also convinced that in this landscape there's a good chance of seeing a rare red grouse in the heather.

Botanists have recorded green hairstreak butterflies basking on bilberry in the summer sunshine here and report that this place is also home to a great variety of lichens, ferns and mosses. We are already impressed with the lush carpet of bluebells on the woodland floor and make a mental note to return later in the year to appreciate the array of autumnal colours.

In case of any debate, the sign beside the lakes clearly says 'Cold deep water'. Lenamore is the upper lake, and in the right shoes the gravel path is easy to walk on. From the car park it follows a figure-of-eight formation, so you can walk in either direction. There are benches conveniently placed to rest a while in the peaceful setting of these beautiful lakes, with only the sheep and the ever-watchful Sperrins for company.

There's a mystical dimension to these dark waters, which is more tangible on the day we visit because of the grey skies and gathering clouds. It's a romantic landscape too, that international visitors especially would lap up and, closer to home, courting couples might favour. Dot has already made firm plans for a return visit, though it may be less to do with Terry and more with what she says has made her day. From near the reedbed at the end of the lower lake, singing in full and lustrous voice for his three-woman audience, is a swaggering sedge warbler.

This little beauty ranks among Dot's favourite birds and the Gortin Lake serenade is the first one Dot has been treated to this year. Her tea and carefully packed picnic will taste all the sweeter after this stand-out performance. But she says the best may be yet to come at a canal in Strabane. In Dot we trust.

© Stephen Maxwell

Sedge warblers (12.5cm) have a streaked head and darker, bolder streaks on their back and wings. They have a creamy-white eyestripe and a sharp bill, ideal for catching flies. With a rounded tail, sedge warblers can be hard to find in the thick undergrowth or in the reedbeds near water, which they favour. Their song is a continuous series of musical, chattering notes. Often they fly vertically upwards, descending rapidly with outspread wings and tail in a show of bravado, hoping to attract a mate. Very quickly, they disappear into the nearest cover and resume their song. In full voice, their distinctive red gape can be seen. They begin to arrive from Africa in April and May to breed here. Like most migrating warblers, the males arrive first to find and set up their territory and then begin to sing for the soon-to-appear females.

I never fully understood the importance that my amazing mother placed on being able to hear the birdsong in every place she lived. Age and wisdom have taught me that it can be the busyness of life that blocks the birdsong out. An unexpected turn on the road led me to a quieter place where I traded the alarm clock for the dulcet tones of the dawn chorus. And now I understand.

CATHERINE MORGAN

A Fisher King in Strabane

My late grandparents lived beside the Ballinderry River in County Tyrone, where a kingfisher family had also made its home. The excitement I felt at seeing the flash of turquoise is still a warm memory. A couple of years ago I saw a kingfisher on the banks of the river at Antrim Castle Gardens and I was immediately transported back to that magical time and place of my childhood.

PAULA MCINTYRE, CHEF AND BROADCASTER

As you would expect, kingfishers are very fond of canals and rivers. Fishing is a daily task and, naturally, they choose to live near this important part of their food chain. This bobby-dazzler of a bird is most industrious early in the morning, when it's hungry after the long night, or after heavy rainfall when pickings are plentiful. We have missed the breakfast show, but the showers have been frequent and heavy, so we live in hope and strike out for the Strabane Canal at Ballymagorry.

Having overshot the runway once or twice, we are relieved when one woman and her dog reset our course precisely, to the Greenlaw Road and ultimately the Strabane Canal. There are windy lanes and there are windy lanes. In this case, no oncoming traffic was a blessing that we accepted gratefully.

The Strabane Canal – a six and a half kilometre stretch of water that connected Strabane to the River Foyle and went on from there to the Foyle Port in Londonderry – opened in 1796 and closed in 1962. The Marquis of Abercorn, who first conceived of the canal, thought it would encourage industrial and commercial development in Strabane and the surrounding area. Despite the fact that most of it was within his estates, an Act of Parliament was required to authorise the building of the waterway, which cost the tidy sum of £11,858.

The canal started in the tidal waters of Lough Foyle at Leck, about ten miles upstream from Derry, leaving the Foyle just above its junction with the Burn Dennet River, before entering Crampsie's Lock. The main water supply came from a stream which entered the canal above Devine's Lock.

Work on the canal began in 1791 under the engineering guidance of John Whally from Coleraine. Most of it was completed within twelve months, but some of the trickier work on the locks and the challenging junction with the Foyle resulted in the entire project not being completed until 1795.

To celebrate the official opening on 21 March 1796, there were bonfires and fireworks. Invited guests and locals ate at the Abercorn Arms and, by all accounts, enjoyed the generous supply of beer courtesy of a free bar.

Ballymagorry District & Development Association are rightly proud of the history and heritage of their area. They have developed a circular walking route with a recently added loop that takes in a restored section of the Strabane Canal. Even before we get our bearings, Dot and I are suitably impressed. The car park is surrounded by trees, hawthorn bushes and there are wide open fields on both sides of the canal. There are kissing gates at Devine's Lock and further gates along the route, leading to spectacular views of the River Foyle and east Donegal.

Savouring the new territory, Dot takes on the guise of a gifted musician who plays by ear. Instantly, her finely tuned auditory sense picks up willow warbler, chiffchaff, blackcap and, not to be outdone by Gortin Forest Park, a trio of sedge warblers who are crooning contentedly in the old overgrown shrubs on the banks of the canal. So far, no kingfishers, but we live in hope.

As we dander towards the old wooden lock gates, we hear the flap of a heron's wings, even though we can't properly see this hulking specimen yet. Dot says herons are a modern version of pterodactyls and she's mightily impressed by their ability to nest in the tops of high trees in spite of their unwieldy shape and size.

It's hard not to be transfixed by these long-legged, long-necked and long-beaked birds, with their distinctive slow-flapping wingbeats and curved wings. It is a privilege to watch them arrive at their selected spot in the water and stand with an angler's patience, fishing for hours on end.

Either this particular heron is not keen on two women with two sets of binoculars trained on him or he's fussy about his fishing stand along the canal. We are almost hypnotised as he lands and takes off three times, selecting a different vantage point along the water each time. That this oversized creature can lift and fly at all is a miracle in itself and once again testament to Mother Nature's ingenuity. Dot says they manage it by flying with heads and necks tucked in and legs jutting out beyond their tails. She also thinks our Tyrone heron may be a youngish bird, unsure of his territory as yet and learning as he goes.

We leave him in peace and Dot wonders why we don't see any mallard ducks as the canal has good areas of long grasses for cover. She's puzzled and stops in her tracks. I follow suit. Looking from one side of the path to the other and studying the grass intently, she explains that the flattened grass is a surefire sign that an otter may have crossed here. The mallard ducks are no dozers and have had good reason to reject this place as a nesting site.

As the sun continues to glint through the trees and hedgerows, it's easy to see why the locals, at least, make the most of this beautiful walk. There are seats peppered along the route, and at the end of

Heron © Paul Hunter

the path, where the canal joins Lough Foyle, there are mute swans, cormorants and more herons.

Dot remains convinced that kingfishers frequent this particular place as it provides at least two of their requirements – water and fish. We agree that for the next Tyrone trip we may need to pack a bag and stay a night or two. Dot says Terry is already working on a special bird-friendly motorbike with a sidecar for his favourite bird woman and her would-be trainee.

© *Chris Henry*

Herons (90–98cm) are large water birds with long legs, a long neck and an elongated dagger-sharp bill. They have a striking black crest, trailing breast feathers and a grey, black and white body. The wings are made to match their size, and in flight this ungainly bird could be a creature from another world.

Herons have the patience of saints and can be seen standing at shallow water for long periods of time ready to stab their prey and swallow it whole in their oversized beaks. These impressive birds nest on the tops of tall trees and in colonies on a platform which they construct using sticks. When they fly, they draw their necks back and with slow beats of their large, arched, black-tipped grey wings, quietly fly away.

© Alan Gallagher

Kingfishers (15cm) are miniature supermodels in the bird world, and, though tiny, move at the speed of light. A brilliant flash of blue and the kingfisher is out of sight in the blink of an eye. The crown and upperparts are blue and they have an aquamarine-barred black rump with a white throat and orange-red breast to colour coordinate with their short orange legs. The male and female are the same size and colour except for a hint of orange lipstick on the females lower beak. They are always found near water and are masters in the art of camouflage and of fishing.

As a child, I would look at a bird and, intuitively, I believed that I knew if it was happy, sad, mischievous, kind or cantankerous. Of course, as I got older, I forgot all that sentimental nonsense. Then, today, as I was sitting in the garden, feeling more than a little lost and sorry for myself, I saw a very stern blackbird, perched on a high branch, head to the side, a look of concern in its eyes as it watched me; and somehow I just knew it was thinking, 'For goodness sake, would you ever catch yourself on!'

KEITH BEATTIE, HISTORIAN

SUMMER

Arctic tern © Stephen Maxwell

A sea stack on Rathlin Island
© *Terry Goldsmith*

Comings and Goings
on Rathlin Island

Whether it's the call of a gull that reminds you of holidays and ice cream along the coast, the hoot of an owl that ushers in memories of wooded walks and autumnal nights, or the pleasant chirping of songbirds that takes you back to simple happy moments from childhood, few sounds can bring you back into a moment or a place in time like birdsong. Take a deep breath, close your eyes and listen to the songs outside your door. You never know where they might take you.

CONLETH MULLAN, ULSTER HISTORICAL FOUNDATION

Gazing across the six-mile stretch of sea that separates Rathlin Island from Ballycastle, it's hard not to feel a sense of awe and wonder. The distinctive 'L' shape of this prehistoric, volcanic land mass is striking, and when you do visit, it's well within the capacity of even a novice walker to trek across the four miles that will take you from one side of the island to the other.

Rathlin is revered by birdwatchers from around the world and every year thousands of international visitors descend on Northern Ireland's only inhabited offshore island and home to one of the UK's largest seabird colonies, including hundreds of puffins.

Dot and I had made a plan to combine our day in Ballycastle with a trip over on the ferry to Rathlin. But, in the blink of an eye, the weather changed and the sea looked angry and foreboding. Before long, word came that the ferries weren't running. We knew that even if one left from the mainland, there was always the chance that it might not be able to bring us back, and while there are certainly worse places to be marooned than Rathlin, Dot and I didn't take the chance.

Dot has spent many days and nights on Rathlin and nips across at least two or three times a year, usually in the summer season when the RSPB need people to help with the large numbers of visitors who head to the spectacular viewing point at the Rathlin West Light Seabird Centre. Dot usually goes with one of her keen birdwatching friends, in a car packed with food, telescope, binoculars, tripod, jumpers, coats, walking boots and, crucially, teabags. The bus meets the ferry at the small harbour in Church Bay and nimbly makes its way along the windy roads, dropping the volunteers at the RSPB cottage. After a quick cuppa and a toss-up for the comfiest bed, it's straight to work.

Rathlin West Light Seabird Centre
© Terry Goldsmith

Guillemots and kittiwakes © Paul Hunter

From mid-April onwards, Rathlin is alive with the sight and sound of seabirds – guillemots, razorbills, kittiwakes, fulmars, shags and perhaps most popular of all, puffins. May, June and July is by far the best time to visit the island. The birds gather en masse on the tall cliff stacks, vying to get the best nest sites. This is a stunning visual spectacle, and the sound and smell equally unforgettable. Birders compete to spot the first chicks hatching on bare ledges, in full view of the captivated spectators.

Dot remembers one particular volunteering trip when the weather was so bad on Rathlin that the ferry couldn't make the return journey to Ballycastle. But it didn't stop her from enjoying the sanctuary that this island also provides and delighting in up close and personal time with her feathered friends. Undaunted by wind or rain and kitted out from top to toe in tried and tested waterproof gear, Dot selected the best seat in the house and settled down to watch fulmars nesting beside the safety fence that surrounds the sea bird centre.

The razorbills preferred one of the other cliff stacks and Dot was enthralled by the constant chatter between the families. By the next day, the weather had improved and many families arrived with youngsters all agog at the prospect of seeing a real live puffin.

Thankfully there were hundreds of puffins to see, so Dot had no trouble lining one up for the excited wee ones to peek at through the telescope. She says it's their reaction that always makes her day. When the children say, 'I see it, I see it', her work is done and she's a happy birder and Rathlin guide.

The three-mile walk back to the cottage at the end of her shift is a joy. Refreshingly quiet and with barely a car in sight, there are just a few cows chewing the cud on the slopes of the wide open fields. Meadow pipits dance in the wind and greylags are relaxing in the lake. After dinner at the cottage, it's off to the pub, not least of all because it's the best place on the island to get a good phone signal. Despite numerous trips to Rathlin over many years, Dot never tires of spending time on the island. All too soon, it's time to get the ferry back to Ballycastle and an entirely different way of life.

While it's hugely important for breeding seabirds, Rathlin Island is also home to Northern Ireland's only pair of breeding chough and more recently to corncrake. In 2021, four calling male corncrakes were recorded on the island for the first time in more than forty years.

The corncrake is a secretive bird, known for its distinctive *crex-crex* call. It is one of Northern Ireland's rarest birds and is on the red list, which means it is a bird of high conservation concern, with numbers that have been in sharp decline since the 1980s. Rathlin is the only place in Northern Ireland that is now home to this species, and the RSPB here has worked hard to create the right habitat for this remarkable corncrake comeback. At least three birds have been heard in nettle beds created over the last decade by staff and volunteers aiming to attract corncrakes to the field margins of Church Bay. The hope is to achieve a sustainable population of these extraordinary birds, with four or five pairs regularly breeding. Corncrakes have two broods – the first in June and the second in late July or early August. After the second brood hatches in August or September, the birds will migrate back to Africa.

Liam McFaul is the RSPB'S warden on Rathlin and monitors the corncrakes. RSPB NI works to protect the precious species in habitats across Northern Ireland, and has been operating here for over fifty years. It has more than 11,000 members, around 60 employees, 300 volunteers and 10 reserves, including Rathlin's West Light Seabird Centre.

Liam grew up on Rathlin and remembers a time when corncrakes could always be heard singing in the fields and could be found across the whole island. Over time, he saw a decline, until eventually the birds just weren't there anymore. 'So much of our work,' he told Dot, 'has been about trying to turn the tide. We've worked closely with landowners. With all the habitat work, we eventually had one bird coming back, then a few years later two birds, then three and now it's up to four. We've been working towards this for a long time.'

A Northern Ireland Environment Agency corncrake grant scheme is in place on Rathlin and is administered by RSPB NI. The scheme works with farmers to ensure their lands remain safe for these protected birds.

Corncrakes are easily spooked, so the advice is not to get close to the birds, which are by and large on private land. It is vitally important they are not disturbed and that this sensitive conservation effort is not compromised.

Since there's no hope of our own planned trip to Rathlin, Dot tells me another story, a reminder that every visit to Rathlin is an adventure. On one of her summer volunteering stints, a heavy fog had set in and lasted for most of the day. Undaunted, Dot finetuned her sense of smell and hearing, secure in the knowledge that there were over a thousand guillemots nesting on the stacks of rocks just in front of the viewing platform and around the cliff edges.

Intermittent breaks in the murkiness revealed bundles of grey fluffy fulmar, kittiwake and razorbill babies sitting perilously close to the edge of the cliffs. Before long, the puffins ventured out of their burrows and Dot did a quick count. She got to thirty-two and then noticed a peregrine falcon surveying the scene from a grassy bank at the bottom of the cliff. Dot knew exactly what was going to happen. There was only one thing on the falcon's mind – and it wouldn't end well for at least one of the puffins.

Onlookers asked Dot why this formidable bird of prey seemed to be immovable. She encouraged them to simply watch. When the moment was right, the peregrine falcon suddenly pounced on a puffin just as it emerged from the burrow. Amid the gasps of shock, Dot explained that this is what this species is designed to do. Birds of prey feed on meat and they too have families to provide for. This is nature in action.

Perversely, the fog finally lifted as Dot and the other volunteers left to catch the ferry back to Ballycastle. The bird whisperer quietly hoped that they might miss this crossing and have an unplanned but welcome sleepover. One day is never enough and from the boat, in keeping with tradition, she always looks back to ensure a return visit.

But it's not going to be today and, reluctantly, we pack up and head for home. Rathlin ranks high on Dot's list of best birding spots and outstanding places and already she's planning our next trip there.

© Chris Henry

Puffins are hard to miss, with their black back and white underparts, distinctive black head, large pale cheeks and tall, flattened, brightly coloured bills. These trademark bills allow the birds to really show off during the breeding season. In winter they sport a much duller beak. Their comical appearance is heightened by red and black eye-markings and bright orange legs.

Their short wings are adapted for swimming and they have an ingenious underwater flying technique. By flapping their wings they can dive to depths of sixty metres in search of fish. In the air, they beat their wings rapidly, up to four hundred times per minute in swift flight, often flying low over the ocean's surface. Sometimes referred to as 'a clown among seabirds', the puffin is one of the world's favourite birds.

For most of the year, puffins bob about at sea, returning to land to breed in April. Between April and July they are hard at work raising their pufflings. By August, the puffins and their charges are back off out to sea.

Most puffins start breeding when they are five years old and often live for more than two decades. Some young, inexperienced birds may change mates after breeding failures but most will mate with the same partner for many years.

Having spent more than thirty years around the seas of Belfast Lough, it wasn't until I had a group of fishermen out in my boat near the Gobbins cliffs that I noticed the noise and smell of the nesting birds. We moved closer and suddenly I was excited by these great seabirds – guillemots, razorbills, kittiwakes, little puffins just sitting on the grass and fulmars gliding above them. Something about the beauty of nature awakened in me that day and I'll never forget it.

BRIAN MEHARG

Dancing Hawks
in Coconut Lane

What a wonderful way to start the day – one very cute little blue tit perched on the windowsill looking in as if to say, 'Good morning.' And then almost every day at lunchtime, a blackbird having his daily dip in the birdbath. Isn't nature truly wonderful.

Thelma McAleese

In 2013, after twenty-five years working and living in Belfast, I upped sticks and moved back to my homeplace of Portstewart. Despite regular weekend visits with my parents, I soon realised as a permanent resident that much had changed from my last tenure here, as a youngster in the seventies and eighties.

On regular walks to parts of the town I hadn't been to in years, it didn't take long to deduce that Portstewart had at least doubled in size, with houses and apartments in fields and green spaces where my brothers and I had played when we were children.

The founder of the town in the late eighteenth century was a man called John Cromie. His maternal ancestors were the Stewarts of Ballylesse and, among other things, he built an imposing mansion called Cromore House. My first move was to a house that backed on to a narrow country lane on the outskirts of Portstewart, in close proximity to this much grander and older dwelling.

This Georgian-style building is surrounded by skyscraper-tall, ancient sycamore trees. It's the perfect environment for birds of prey who can make their nests as high as eighty feet up, within the security of the uppermost branches. Buzzards or 'dancing hawks', as they are also known, are particularly fond of this type of environment.

The waggishness of these clever birds consumed my first summer back in Portstewart. Every morning, I made for the best upstairs vantage point to admire what I came to call my Portstewart eagles.

Through my binoculars, which Dot was very pleased I'd now acquired, and a telescope my brother gave me as a birthday present, I observed that the buzzards had very thick, stocky legs. It occurred to me that maybe these were the kind of legs I might have developed as a youngster if I hadn't stopped playing football. That's what our neighbour used to tell me anyway.

Regardless, I was totally transfixed by the legs of these well-built, handsome birds, who can perch, stock still, on top of a gatepost or telegraph pole for hours on end and yet, in an instant, can run very quickly across a large field to pounce on whatever might be on the menu that day. If these birds played rugby, never mind football, the dancing hawks squad would present a formidable line-out and be

Buzzard © Denis Chambers

a tough scrum to crack. When they don't resemble a rugby team, they take on the guise of regimental sentries keeping a very close eye on their patch.

As the summer wore on, my fixation with this ornithological convocation showed no sign of abating. It was time to call in the expert. I'd been keeping Dot in touch with the comings and goings and I think she was getting a kick out of my growing fascination.

On the appointed day, an early morning weather check indicated an all-too-familiar intermittent wet and gusty July day; not enough to put either of us off and, given their extended summer holiday in Portstewart, not bad enough to worry my increasingly large, back-door buzzard family. Dot says she was intrigued from the moment she heard me say excitedly, 'You have to come up and see these big birds running back and forward in the field behind my house.'

Fortuitously, Dot arrives just after a shower of rain, which she says the buzzards will like because the field will be wet and the hunting easier. As we wander down one of the few narrow country lanes left in Portstewart, where two cars would struggle for room, it dawns on me that this is one of the highest places above sea level in the town – another reason why it's so fiercely windy here when it may not be at the bottom of the lane or on the main road.

Dot immediately appreciates the hedgerows on either side of what I have christened 'Coconut Lane', because of the beautiful aroma provided by the canary-yellow whin bushes. She says thickets like this provide great cover for robins, dunnocks and house sparrows, who, incidentally, are delighted to see their favourite twitcher and offer her a rapturous welcome.

As we come to a gap in the hedge beside the field, sure enough there are eight burly buzzards hard at work, walking, running and hopping back and forward across the undulating, recently cut grassland. The lure of small bugs, worms, mice and anything that moves, accounts for their constant vigilance.

The dancing hawks are rarely off-duty at this time of the year. In an instant, it becomes clear how well this name suits them. Were either of us musically inclined and able to strike up a tune, the buzzards would indeed look like they were dancing to a newly released Blakely/McAleese composition.

Perhaps in a bid to woo Dot, my other feathered friends, the seagulls, also put in an appearance, as do the local crows. Each species seems entirely unperturbed by the other's presence in this large, food-rich pasture, content with their own patch and happy to mind their own business. Dot says there is room for everyone. In this regard, she believes that Mother Nature is a genius at maintaining perfect harmony. As is often the case, we would do well to learn from her example.

Before too long, the clouds have gathered and the sky has darkened. We think it's a good idea to adjourn the meeting, have tea and freshly baked scones back at my house and do the science bit there. That's what I told Dot anyway – though I'm not sure she believed me about the scones.

One of the best things for birds is a good, thick, tall native hedge with hawthorn and blackthorn, dogr rose, willow, crab apple and wild cherry and elder, rowan, ivy and brambles for blackberries. hedges provide shelter and food; somewhere to live and breed and feel safe for all kinds of birds and other wildlife.

JILLY DOUGAN, GARDENER AND BEEKEEPER

© Denis Chambers

Buzzards or dancing hawks can reach 55cm in height, so these birds of prey fall into the large category. They are a familiar site on the top of telegraph poles and trees. They sport an upright stance with heavy, dark brown underparts and a rounded body. In flight, the large broad wings show a white underside and white belly. Buzzards can often be seen gently soaring in circles, high in the sky in the rising thermals, wings back and pointed, with the tail fanned, acting as a reliable rudder and steering wheel. Their carrying call is an unmistakable *kiew, kiew* and, depending on the wind direction, can be heard clearly, well beyond their chosen fields.

Like most birds of prey, or 'raptors', they have a hooked beak, large yellow legs and killer feet to match. Nesting sites can be found in woodlands at the tip-tops of trees, or on cliff edges. Their favourite prey is rabbits, but buzzards have excellent eyesight and this means they are also very good hunters when it comes to mice and carrion.

The 'dancing hawk' moniker is a reference to their amusing way of running or hopping across the fields hunting for mice and large worms. This kind of prey requires less prowess and energy than that needed to outwit well-tuned-in rabbits, with their large ears and sharp teeth. In summer, when they're not roosting, buzzards spend hours on end in the freshly cut grassy fields of their chosen territory.

Dot to the Rescue

Leaving food out in our yard, carefully and lovingly
prepared, then running inside to watch hungry
birds descend to tuck into their unexpected lunch;
surprised and delighted equally, taking my duty of
care very seriously – that's what birds mean to me,
a remembrance of my childhood.

ÁINE TONER, FEATURES EDITOR,
Belfast Telegraph & Sunday Life

It's no exaggeration to say that Dot has a special relationship with birds. Most of her adult life has been spent in the pursuit of knowledge about these feathery creatures, which in turn has enabled her to recognise their habits and foibles and to develop a unique understanding of how birds think and operate.

She remains modest in this regard, reiterating that she is not an academic birder, but rather an instinctive enthusiast. For my money, she's like a doctor with a good bedside manner – someone in whom you have full confidence and who leaves you feeling much better. This is a story she told me about what happened one summer in her garden in Bangor.

It had been an unusually hot summer and Dot was keeping an extra-close eye on the blue tits nesting in her garden. The previous February, as she always does at that time of year, she had cleared out the two nest boxes, one attached to the fence, the other to one of the trees. She says the best way to do this is by wearing a glove, opening the box and taking away all of the old nest.

In her experience, occasionally one of the young chicks may become a casualty of a large brood due to its inability to compete with larger siblings in the fight to get food from the parents. Through trial and error, Dot has learned that nests can be treasure troves of information. If you know how to interpret it, what can be gleaned from the nest is invaluable.

Bird boxes are used mostly by blue tits. The entry and exit point should be between 25 and 27mm in diameter. The ideal location for them is on fences, trees, ivy or bushes, and in a place that offers some degree of shelter from the full glare of the sun or torrential rain. The birds are happiest when they can come and go easily, swooping through trees and bushes to spend some time indoors.

That summer, in the grounds of Blakely manor, a pair of blue tits had been busy bringing in old grass and tiny bits of moss to line the new nest. The construction of the nest happens in no time at all, and before long Dot was in her favourite position, watching one bird in particular making regular visits.

This behaviour means that the female is sitting on the eggs. Three weeks later, both parents were going back and forth, with fighter-pilot precision, straight into the box, mouths laden with tiny flies to feed their young.

Dot's chosen spot for her daily birdwatching fix is about six feet from the box. Her birds know her very well and don't give off or get upset by her presence. If that were to happen she would have no qualms about moving away to ensure their comfort and wellbeing. If birds feel threatened, there is a chance they will abandon the nest, though this would be unusual as the bond with the young is immediate, and strengthened once they start calling for food.

After hatching, Dot reckoned there were five young blue tits in the nest. It's never a good idea to open the box to check. When the youngsters are three weeks old, they are ready to fledge, but Dot's instinct was telling her that all was not well, and in that very warm

summer, as the temperatures continued to soar, she was convinced something was amiss. Not least because the babies had stopped calling for sustenance.

Close scrutiny revealed that both parents were coming back with precious little in the way of food – barely a beakful of tiny greenflies. Dot also deduced that the older birds were agitated, chattering frantically almost as if they were trying to tell their faithful friend that something was definitely wrong. And then the eureka moment. Like the pieces of a jigsaw, Dot put it together and the picture emerged. The babies were quiet because they were too hot as a result of the sun beating down on the box. And because of the heat, the local food supply had died back and food had become scarce.

In an instant, Dot disappeared and returned from her house with the solution. With no time to lose, a black umbrella was arranged above the box, in full view of the initially bemused parents. As soon as this innovative operation was complete, the parents entered the nest again. And Dot went to the shop.

Returning with a quarter pound of live, white wax worms in a paper bag, she duly placed them in a coconut shell within close range of the nest box. Fingers crossed, she stood back and watched in grateful relief as the parents made for the booty. Within seconds of the parents entering and then exiting the nest, relieved of their nourishing worms, Dot heard the youngsters calling again. This enterprising feeding arrangement continued until a peaceful silence returned and the well-fed youngsters were safely tucked up and out for the count.

The whole enterprise was so successful that Dot continued it for the next fortnight. It even attracted the attention of a great tit who wanted in on the action and ended up with his own personal coconut shell on the other side of the garden.

For the rest of the summer, by way of a thank you, the blue tit parents greeted Dot warmly every morning. Trust between humans and birds is not easily won and once gained should be guarded like a precious jewel.

© Michael Graham

Four out of the five baby blue tits survived that summer. Had it not been for Dot's intuition and swift action, it might well have been a different story.

The birds in the trees of my back garden are like nature's choir. The blackbirds, robins and blue tits may be hidden from view by the leaves, but their wonderful individual songs fill the air and they are never out of tune. It's always an uplifting musical experience.

DONNA TRAYNOR, TV PRESENTER

Terns, Terns, Terns
in Groomsport

I enjoy walking along both the coastal and woodland
paths in Groomsport because this allows me to hear
and see lots of different birds, which is just wonderful.

ERNIE PRITCHARD

For almost a hundred years it was possible to get the train to Groomsport in County Down. Well, almost. The line from Newtownards to Donaghadee opened in 1861 and did have a stop near Groomsport. The trouble was that it was several miles from the village. The halt was renamed Groomsport Road but, sadly, like many other railway lines across the country, it was closed in the 1950s.

In Irish, Groomsport means 'port of the gloomy servant'. My feeling is that this character must have had a predisposition towards a negative outlook on life as the village is a natural beauty with very little gloom or doom on display. It's just two miles from Bangor, on the southern shores of Belfast Lough and the northern tip of the Ards Peninsula.

In the seventeenth and eighteenth centuries, the harbour in Groomsport was important enough to have its own customs house. A further claim to fame is that the ill-fated ship, *Eagle Wing*, set out from here in 1636. It was the first emigrant ship to leave these shores for the New World. There were 140 men, women and children on board, all making the fearful voyage to North America. After eight weeks at sea, enduring ferocious weather, the journey was abandoned and *Eagle Wing* returned home.

Throughout the nineteenth century, the fishing fleet in the village expanded and a lifeboat station was built in the sheltered bay. As well as fishing, farming and loom-weaving were the means by which people made a living. The arrival of the railway made Groomsport much more accessible and, slowly but surely, it became a popular tourist destination.

Two cottages at Cockle Row have been authentically restored and now offer a unique glimpse into life for fishermen and their families at the beginning of the last century. No doubt those early fishermen would cast a quizzical look in the direction of the keen sailors and open-water swimmers who now frequent the waters around this largely unchanged village. Then and now, it's a picture-postcard place, oozing tranquility and charm in equal measure.

A group of rocks known as Cockle Island are within a stone's throw of the village and also form part of Ballymacormick Point, which is a designated Area of Special Scientific Interest. The National Trust have looked after this stunning section of the County Down

Sandwich tern © Stephen Maxwell

Golden plovers © Denis Chambers

coastline since 1952. It's a particularly important site for breeding terns who arrive here between April and September and Dot says there's a thriving population of black-headed gulls too.

On these tiny, rocky, grass-covered islands, there can be over one hundred terns fighting, feeding and mating at any one time. The sight and sound of these birds as they lift, turn and come back down to the scrape of a nest is quite a performance to behold. The British Trust for Ornithology has two cameras on the island enabling people to watch and learn about the terns from one of the Cockle Row cottages.

Given the close proximity of Cockle Island to Groomsport, and as the sun was splitting the stones on this August day, had Dot and I been so inclined, we could have been swimming over to meet the terns in person. But neither of us are sea swimmers, although we do share the same respect and love for the sea. Today, Dot has her sights firmly fixed on Ballymacormick Point, a bustling, busy place for birds in the summer and one she knows every square inch of.

It's two miles from where Dot lives in Bangor and she often walks along the convenient path between the two places, which is managed by the Northern Ireland Environment Agency.

She's confident that today we will find whitethroat, chiffchaff, willow and sedge warblers. In winter, this rocky, gorse-covered, rough-grass headland is a nerve centre for golden plover, redshank, dunlin, ringed plover, turnstone, curlew and oystercatchers. On repeated visits, and with the help of her trusty binoculars, Dot has also recorded stonechats, reed buntings, linnets, blackbirds, robins, wrens and meadow pipits, all happily at home in this natural ornithological paradise. For good measure, herons nest in the tall trees near the

Ballyholme side of the path to Ballymacormick.

Beside the coastal path, when the harbour is in low tide, terns and black-headed, common, herring, lesser, and great black-backed gulls can be found, bathing and feeding in the small river coming out to the sea. High water in the lough will present fishing terns, black guillemot, shelduck, eider and red-breasted mergansers. Today, the terns are out of the harbour, fishing, and we are treated to the sight of them whizzing past the headland with their excitable young screaming alongside them. The shelduck and mallard prefer the peace and quiet of the inlet where they can feed happily in the mud.

This fleeting visit to Groomsport has guaranteed my return and reminded me that my maternal grandmother was a woman of excellent taste. She and my grandfather rented a house here for a month every summer in the 1930s and '40s, when my mother and uncle were small children. Far from being 'gloomy', this is a port that wears an infectious smile that my grandparents certainly appreciated. There's no reason to think that this won't be the case for many generations to come

© Stephen Maxwell

The **sandwich tern** (41cm) is the largest of the terns. It has a black forehead and crown, with a shaggy crest and a black bill with a yellow tip. It has short black legs and the male and female look alike. The body is mostly white, with sharp heavy-looking light-grey wings. Terns are built for speed and fly with their head bowed, watching constantly for sand eels or small fish. They hover and dive into the sea to catch their prey. The young can fly at about five weeks. In the winter, they prefer the warmer seas found near South Africa.

© Stephen Maxwell

The **common tern** (36cm) is smaller than the sandwich tern. It has a black forehead, with a red, black-tipped bill and longer legs that are a dullish rust-red colour. The male and female look the same: both have pale white bodies, long neat grey wings with a translucent patch, and lengthy tail streamers. This is perhaps why they are nicknamed sea swallows. They can also be found on inland lakes.

© Stephen Maxwell

The **arctic tern** (36cm) is similar in size and wing colour to the common tern. It has a black forehead, a bright red bill and shorter red legs. The arctic tern has a shorter, forked tail with long pointed wings. It too spends the winter in warmer, southern-hemisphere oceans.

My earliest bird memory is the cooing of wood pigeons. I must have been in a cot at home in our cottage at Mahee Island during World War Two when I heard them and paid attention. So they are the sound of my childhood and instil the same pleasure now that I'm in my second childhood!

JULIE MACKIE

Flight School in Ballyness

*Birdwatching with friends and sharing a flask,
sandwiches and bird facts is a great way to spend a
day out in natural surroundings. Exploring field and
woodland, river and shoreline is in itself a delight,
but looking for and identifying the different species
of birds found in these various environments by
their appearance and habits is a very rewarding and
fascinating interest.*

JOHN RICHIE

As with all newborn babies, a month makes a big difference in a swan's young life. Four weeks on from our first trip to Ballyness in County Antrim to meet the cygnets and the word is that already significant changes have occurred. We are excited – at least I am. Dot has been worrying about them. She explains that young swans are very vulnerable for the first few months of their lives. There are many threats to their survival and it's crucial that they learn quickly how to feed themselves, stay warm and recognise and avoid dangerous situations, especially attacks from other male swans.

In only a few weeks the cygnets are noticeably larger and heavier. The little bundles of fluff have lost much of their initial down and already have a few grey and white feathers, and we can see the beginnings of their beautiful, long necks. Dot and I are both of the opinion that there's no such thing as an ugly duckling or an ugly swan, though the moral of Hans Christian Andersen's story is a good one.

Both parents are now encouraging the cygnets to move around the pond on their own. Two are feeding on the extra grain that David, the former owner of the caravan park, leaves out for them every morning to supplement the natural food in the small lake that has to be shared among all the residents.

As Dot surveys the situation, the cygnets float around to where we are, one in particular calling all the while to its parents. But the pen and cob stay near the big island in the centre, apparently unperturbed by the persistent cries of one of their brood. Dot says that this is unusual and that, as a rule, the adults normally respond to a cygnet who may be in distress. She deduces that this feeble-looking, scrawnier cygnet is the runt of the family and will get no special attention from either parent. It's a hard lesson to witness but a necessary one for this youngster if it is to have any chance of surviving in the wild on its own.

As the cygnets put on weight, they will have more energy, become more active and will be able to stay warm more easily, and will therefore be less inclined to look to their parents for heat and food. Mum and Dad will continue to maintain a vigilant eye, albeit from a distance, but Dot says this watchfulness will lessen slowly but surely over the next six months.

Swans take great care of their appearance – being this beautiful takes work – and they can often be seen simply standing and preening their sensational white feathers. They're also keen on shakedowns, which has nothing to do with a con trick and more to do with personal grooming: flapping their wings back and forth helps to get rid of any dust and grime that may have built up in their most precious asset.

In the early days, after they left the nest, the cygnets slept on their parents' back; now that they are bigger, it's safer for them to sleep on the water. If we'd been here first thing this morning, Dot says, we'd have heard the cygnets' early, contented calls, signifying that all is well and another day has dawned. This time, we leave in the sincere hope that the little, struggling cygnet will survive until our next visit.

The cygnets are now about five months old and Olive has been in touch to let Dot know that she thinks flight school has begun. For all young swans, the urge to fly is instinctive and irresistible. In the months that have passed since our last visit, Olive reports that preening and wing-flapping activity have increased. Dot's theory is that this strengthens their wings to help ensure that the difficult first flight will be a success.

This time, Dot and Terry's friends, Richard and Val, have come too, having been entranced by our reports on the life and times of the Ballyness swans. Over the years, the fab four have spent many great birdwatching days together. They have their excursions down to a fine art now: a picnic, fold-up seats, binoculars, gloves and hats depending on the weather. Regardless of the bird activity, they know that time spent with good friends is always time well spent.

Despite the season, this was definitely a hat and, in my case, oversized anorak day. Dot is undaunted by the weather and when we arrive has only one thing in mind: to count the cygnets and make sure there are still six of them. Her ever-ready binoculars are out and trained on the ponds. The next couple of silent minutes seem like an eternity, but then Dot gives a whoop of delight and pronounces that all the cygnets are present and correct. The runt of the litter has rallied and seems to be holding his own, even if it is in the shadow of his slightly bigger brothers and sisters.

The teenagers, as Dot calls them, are now almost the same size as the parents. Their grey, buff feathers are mixed with new streaks of white, alongside a pinkish-grey bill. Our arrival coincides with the start of their flight lesson. After some calling and last-minute instruction from one parent, class gets underway. While it may resemble organised chaos, the adult swans are firmly in control, overseeing the proceedings and encouraging the young to try, try, and try again. And they do – wings flapping frantically, determined in their clumsy canters along the top of the water, like toddlers attempting to run before they can walk.

Flap, run, flap, run. Repeat. From one side of the pond to the other, back and forth, back and forth. Finally, enough is enough – class is concluded, and it's bathtime. At this stage, the cygnets are well able to upend by themselves, skilfully turning upside down in the water to wash their feathers and dispatch any fluff and dirt. With age, preening becomes ever more important in a swan's life. Even at this youthful stage in their lives, the little swans take to it with gusto and plenty of tomfoolery.

Dot's anxieties about the smaller cygnet have been allayed and she notes that he has been included in all the activities of the day. This, she concludes, means that he's feisty and determined, two qualities that will be imperative if he is to make it on his own in a couple of months' time, when the parents dispatch the young adults and they take flight with strengthened wings and chest muscles.

As we're leaving, a man doing work around the park reminds Dot about a kingfisher that has been spotted near the small river that flows on the other side of the ponds. Our day only gets better when we glimpse a flash of blue that signals the diminutive kingfisher moving among the small branches on the river bank. Dot also spies herons, well camouflaged in the taller trees, but the otter that comes upriver when there's been a lot of rain is nowhere to be seen, though Dot's convinced that some mallard feathers are signs of an earlier visit. The cygnets have lived to fight another day and, with luck, the trainee pilots will decamp before long and the circle of life will continue.

The swans of Ballyness will live long in our hearts and minds. We're tempted by the idea of booking neighbouring caravans for next year. We resolve to come back next spring and wave at any swans in flight in the meantime.

Other Birds at Ballyness

Tree and house sparrows are very much in evidence around the car park at Ballyness. A number of seed feeders have been placed in the bushes and, as the excitable, noisy sparrows congregate to chat and sometimes argue about who's top bird, it's almost as though the hedges are moving. Robins and goldfinches are also keen on this idyllic spot. Listen out for their chirpy and tingling song. There is also at least one yellowhammer that is very much at home in Ballyness, no doubt seduced by the natural charm of this special place. Much like we were.

© Stephen Maxwell

The male **yellowhammer** (16cm) has a bright yellow head and belly, with an orangey-yellow breast. Upperparts are streaked chestnut black. Females are the same, though slightly duller. These birds like open spaces and are found in the countryside, in fields, hedgerows and on telegraph wires. Their song is distinctive and, if vocalised, sounds very like *a little bit of bread and no cheese.* They nest low to the ground, in thick bushes and under hedgerows. Grain and seeds are their food of choice. In the course of her RSPB surveys, Dot has enjoyed watching these birds many times. Comber in County Down is a particularly good place to find them.

Ballyness is an amazing place to see wildlife in action. This is because two people, Olive and David Dunlop, cared enough to create a haven for birds, bees, butterflies and otters. Mother Nature needs a helping hand sometimes.

TERRY BLAKELY

Hidden Gems at Kernohans Lane in Ballymena

It really is the small things in life, like birdwatching and appreciating nature, that bring so much pleasure in life.

Joan Harvey

In my late teens and early twenties, a day out in Ballymena was something I looked forward to. It meant shopping, a taste of independence and that I had my own money to spend. A friend from schooldays lived in Cloughmills and had a groovy old Alfa Romeo to get her back and forth to her course at the technical college in Coleraine. She knew all the good shops in the City of the Seven Towers and, more importantly, when the sales were on.

After one of our shopping trips, we arrived back at her parents' house with what we thought were the coolest outfits on the planet – Rupert the Bear tartan trousers and American baseball jackets to match. We made the case for how much of a bargain they were – only five pounds each! – but it fell on deaf ears and stricken faces.

I'd like to say that we appreciated the green fields that we passed on either side of the A26, en route to our regular shopping sprees but, in truth, neither of us paid much attention to the landscape around us. As is often the case with what's right under your nose, it can take time or a dramatic change in circumstances to remind us of its immense value. By and large, the majority of those green fields are still there, notwithstanding the addition of a new dual carriageway for the vastly increased traffic volume and a flyover for pedestrians.

Fast forward a few years and I'm still keen on bargain-hunting in Ballymena, but I'm even happier to leave the town centre behind and head out along the Broughshane Road to Kernohans Lane. It's now home to the Ecos Centre, an environmental and interpretative centre on 220 acres of council-owned land within the flood plain of the Braid River.

The Ecos Centre and Nature Park officially opened in 2000 to great acclaim. It has more than lived up to what it promised to be – 'an oasis of wildlife close to the heart of Ballymena'. The design of the centre is clever and eco-friendly, and uses the thermal flywheel effect to store energy efficiently. Kevin McCloud would be impressed.

The meadows are grazed by Irish Moiled cattle and in summer the fields are festooned by hundreds of butterflies, fluttering and feasting on the nectar from the wildflowers that thrive in the beautiful meadows here. Dot makes a point of visiting at least once a year, in May or June. She's impressed by the thought that has gone into the design and layout – even down to the bushes in the car park that are now ideal for blackbirds, robins, tits and finches.

Dot is sure that the warblers will be singing and easy to see, because of the wide open reed beds at the lake. Today, though, the stars of the show will be the singing blackcaps. Dot knows they are here as she arrived early to scout the place and has already heard their lovely song as she walked past the small play park near the entrance. They are often referred to as 'northern nightingales' because of their fluting lilt.

Right on cue, as soon as I arrive, silence descends. So we decide to head towards the lake that Dot loves because of the space it provides on and off the water for wildfowl families to bring up their young. Greylags and mallard are dandering about on the grass with their grown-up youngsters, delighting in any food donations from the many fans of the park who walk here every day.

The appeal is all-encompassing. On my regular visits here, I am enveloped in feelings of serenity and calm. With or without the glistening sunshine that we are enjoying today, the mostly flat, eight kilometres of footpath are a gentle guide around this perfectly balanced landscape that really does have something for everyone.

Thankfully, the silent interval is soon over and the judges' favourite, Mr Blackcap, has returned to the stage, in full and fine voice, determined to impress at least one member of the audience and find himself a mate. Lest he think he's hogging the limelight entirely, a couple of dunnocks join in, to the ever-increasing enchantment of the two-woman audience.

Despite his immense performance and musical talent, our blackcap is really quite shy and doesn't appreciate his admirers this morning, so promptly disappears as quickly as he arrived. We walk around to the far side of the lake, which has open reed beds with long grasses and shrubs.

This habitat, Dot advises, is also perfect for nesting birds, stonechats, white throat and her all-time favourite singer, the one and only sedge warbler. Great crested grebes, little grebes, coots and moorhens are also at home near any stretch of calm and sheltered water. Warblers congregate around the paths in the mixed trees and hedgerows, along with goldcrest, long-tailed tits and chiffchaff. Ecos is an ideal breeding refuge for meadow pipits, skylarks and birds like snipe that are in sharp decline in some parts of Northern Ireland. And with such an open landscape there is always the chance of spying a hovering kestrel or a soaring buzzard.

Much has been achieved here in a relatively short space of time. As well as the birds, there are butterflies, bees, insects and a family of otters often seen splashing around on the Braid River and sometimes in the lake.

If we didn't realise it before, today we are both in no doubt that the Ecos Centre is for life, not just for summer. Any nostalgic ideas of shopping that I might have had are now the farthest thing from my mind.

© Paul Hunter

Whitethroat (14cm) arrive here to breed from central Africa between April and October. They have grey heads, a white throat, thin bills, red-brown wings and upperparts, and grey crown feathers that can be raised. This warbler sings from the top of a bush before dancing back and forth while singing to each briar within its sights. It finally disappears to trill to its heart's content in the undergrowth of hawthorn bushes and brambles. Its song is sharp, almost scratchy, and consistently repeats. And repeats.

© Stephen Maxwell

Blackcaps (14cm) are well named as these warblers do indeed wear a black cap, while the female of the species is more disposed to a paler shade of brown. With grey upperparts and light grey underparts, they have a slightly thicker bill than other warblers. Many blackcaps who travel here from Europe now opt to stay here throughout the year. They are shy and choose the thick cover offered by mature hedgerows, brambles and bushes. Their song is rich, flute-like, performed in short bursts and builds to a loud *tacc-tacc* crescendo, resembling the sound of two stones hitting against one another.

I'm certain that I would be a poorer man if I'd never had the privilege of seeing an eagle fly in the wild.

Peter McAleese, film producer

Swallows, Writers and Castles in Enniskillen

Growing up in the countryside in Fermanagh, birds were constant companions. As a youngster I often thought it would be wonderful to have the freedom to fly like them, but I guess the Wright brothers got there first. During the harvesting and haymaking I watched birds foraging in flocks on the ground in the fields beside us.

PETER SHERIDAN

Fermanagh was the county that I knew least well when I started presenting *Your Place and Mine* on BBC Radio Ulster in 1991. And because of that, it was somewhere that I couldn't wait to explore.

It was love at first sight. Even the name, Fermanagh, has a soft, lyrical tone. From the Irish, *Fear Manach*, it translates as Men of Manach, monks possibly, which could be a reference to the county's robust spiritual credentials.

My first visit was to meet Bryan Gallagher, a retired headmaster, as well as a writer and lover of boats, who had spent his whole life living near the shores of Lough Erne. His greeting that day, from an elevated vantage point on his boat by the Round O jetty, just outside Enniskillen, will live long in my memory: 'I'm just scraping *Maeve*'s bottom.' A quick glance at the name painted on the side of the boat confirmed that he was referring to his beloved yacht.

In my mind's eye, I can still see the sunlight shimmering on the water of this beautiful lough. The locals love to say that Lough Erne has an island for every day of the year and I like to think they're right. By now, I've been on quite a few of them. I said a prayer on Devenish, in honour of the monks, and more prayers on Inish Corkish when Pat Doherty's pigs had me surrounded while he splashed through the water to retrieve our boat as it began to drift away.

Lough Erne is huge, and encompasses upper and lower sections. It runs through Enniskillen and, in truth, wherever you are in Fermanagh, you're never really that far away from it. A quick stocktake of my numerous trips to the county includes visits to Lisnaskea, Roslea, Donagh, Tempo, Brookeborough, Kesh, Ederney, Irvinestown, Lisnarrick, Ballinamallard, Maguiresbridge, Lisbellaw, Boho, Florencecourt, Kinawley, Belcoo, Belleek, Garrison, Newtownbutler, Cleenish and Derrygonnelly. And that's not counting the day that I got well and truly lost.

My call to the man I had arranged to meet to tell him that I had was now well and truly lost elicited instructions to keep going, all the way through Big Dog Forest, where there'd be no phone signal, but I'd soon see a white van in a lay-by with the back doors open and that would be him and I'd be there. And he was right and all was well with the world. Faith in Fermanagh is never misplaced.

The stately houses peppered across the county are spectacular too: Florencecourt, Castle Archdale, Crom, Monea, Castle Balfour, Tully Castle and, the king of them all, Enniskillen Castle, which was built in the fifteenth century. It's the oldest building in the town and was the stronghold of the Maguire clan. The chieftain was known as Hugh 'The Hospitable' because of the lavish banquets he used to have there.

Over the years I've lost track of the number of people from this county that I've met and interviewed. Anything I know about Fermanagh is as a result of that. And also because of the good work that consistently happens at Enniskillen Castle Museums. In Irish

Enniskillen Castle
© B. Cleary

the town is *Inis Ceithleann*, which means Cathleen's island. She was a Celtic goddess, wounded in battle by an arrow and then drowned when she tried to swim across the lough. But her memory is alive and well and honoured with numerous references to the story of her island at the Castle Museums.

A day out in Fermanagh also gives me the excuse to bring a packed lunch. At least that's what I used to do until Selwyn Johnston from Headhunters Barber Shop & Railway Museum on Darling Street in the town had other ideas.

It's fair to say that Headhunters Museum is unique. My hunch is that there are very few, if any, places in the United Kingdom where you can have a haircut and immerse yourself in the golden age of steam-train travel at the same time. The haircuts came first, in 1981, when Selwyn's two brothers Gordon and Nigel opened for business. The Railway Museum arrived later, in 2002. The timing was fortuitous, as a local group of railway enthusiasts had formed five years earlier but were unable to find a home for their railway display.

The Johnston family's decision to combine their traditional barber skills with a long-held interest in local railway history has created one of the most fascinating attractions in Northern Ireland. Within its walls on this historic street, there is now a huge collection of Irish railway memorabilia on display, covering the period from the arrival of the railways in this area in 1854 until the closure of the lines in 1957. A fully reconstructed, authentic booking office, complete with a ticket collector, ensures that a visit here accurately recreates a century of railway travel throughout Fermanagh and the border counties. A station master's office and signal box also form part of this lovingly constructed and unrivalled exhibition.

Headhunters is not a museum that stands still. The owners consistently refurbish the displays and artefacts, always with an eye to telling new stories about this period in our shared history. Selwyn is excited that greenways are being explored along the former railway lines from Sligo to Enniskillen and from Enniskillen to Bundoran and Omagh. A review of rail connectivity throughout the island of Ireland, and feasibility studies about reconnecting the west by rail, present the possibility of a return of the railways in this part of the island for the next generation.

Selwyn and I first chatted on the radio in the early 1990s and we've been having great conversations on and off ever since. His knowledge of the railways is surpassed only by his deep affinity and love for his home county. A former High Sheriff and British Empire Medal recipient, his energy is infectious. His favourite coffee shop is The Jolly Sandwich, conveniently located a short distance from the museum. Having sampled a great variety of the fare on offer there, I can confirm that Selwyn is a man of excellent taste. Even if I'm just passing through Enniskillen, more often than not Selwyn appears from nowhere, a bulging brown paper bag in one hand, coffee in the other. 'For the road home,' he says.

It's a lengthy run from Fermanagh to my home on the north coast, so I have earmarked beauty spots in the county where I park up and luxuriate in the landscape that slowly enfolds even the most unsuspecting weary soul. I might stop in the shadow of Cuilcagh, beside the glistening waters of Lough MacNean, or at the castle in Enniskillen overlooking Lough Erne and Castle Island.

It's my belief that places can be very powerful. Since I first set foot in it, Fermanagh has wrapped itself around me like a favourite coat, providing warmth and comfort. It's rare for me to leave any part of this special place without thinking of a line from an old Irish blessing that I've unashamedly adapted, 'May the roads rise to meet you and Fermanagh be always in your heart.'

So it's with great gusto that I set off to meet Dot in the centre of Enniskillen, beside the castle. Dot hasn't spent too much time in the town and so she's not sure what we might encounter but says that, without a doubt, where's there water, there will be birds.

Selwyn has also confirmed that there is definitely a kingfisher along the water's edge here and that they are often spotted along the river pathway, between Portora Royal School gates and Portora Castle. Herons also perch gracefully on the riverbank at Cherry Island, in front of the new South West College. One in particular, Harry the Heron, has become a personality in his own right, with an extensive fan base of locals who regularly walk between the bridges in the town.

In Northern Ireland, Lough Erne is one of the last remaining strongholds of breeding waders. The RSPB's Lower Lough Erne Islands Reserve provides a haven for curlew, lapwing, redshank, snipe and a colony of breeding sandwich terns. The RSPB believes that this abundance of waders might be a result of the lowland wet grassland habitats that stretch all the way around its shores

What we can be sure of today is that there will be 150 beautiful

Harry the Heron © Roy Crawford

swallows in Enniskillen. Brainchild of Arts Over Borders Artistic Director Seán Doran, these golden representations of swallows have been placed on shops and businesses, public buildings and schools throughout the town.

They celebrate the author Oscar Wilde, whose school days at Portora Royal School from 1864 to 1871 are believed to have inspired his short story, 'The Happy Prince'. One of his earliest works, it tells the tale of a statue named The Happy Prince who, day after day, looks down and sees the poverty in the town. He asks the swallow taking shelter at his feet to strip him of his gold and jewels to give to the poor. Locals delight in the belief that this statue is based on Cole's Monument in Forthill Park in the town, which would have been visible from Wilde's elevated school-dormitory window.

The gold-leaf, gilded stainless-steel swallows were created by local visual artists Helen Sharp and Simon Carman and are part of a literary tourism project to help create a permanent link between Wilde and the town. Dot is particularly taken by the notion that visitors to the town will encounter such a powerful message of compassion and will hopefully see the swallows as symbols of optimism and hope.

The picnic tables positioned alongside the water's edge add to Dot's delight and from this comfortable vantage point on this warm, clear day, we settle down to survey the scene in front of us. Stealing the show is a beautiful mute swan with her seven cygnets that Dot judges to be about five weeks old. This swan has been here before and, like the mallard ducks vying for our attention, is highly socialised. She leads her young serenely from one riverbank across the lough to our bank, within touching distance of the jetty.

Dot says swans are well used to the people who frequent this idyllic town-centre outdoor space, but advises caution when it comes to feeding them. In recent years, various research bodies have said that white bread isn't really the best food for wild birds. On balance, Dot thinks it's probably better to give the ducks wet brown bread, seeds or green vegetables. The key thing, she says, is to get children involved

Swans and cygnets on Lough Erne
© Roy Crawford

and interested in birds from an early age, in the hope that they will grow to love, respect and understand them throughout their lives.

The mother and baby swans radiate health and contentment. Sporting a shaggier look than the adults, their little grey wings snugly tucked away, a couple of the cygnets each lift one of their delicate grey legs out of the water and fold it onto the side of their body. The spellbound look on my face elicits a simple and enchanting explanation from Dot: there is no particular reason for this action other than they want to do it. Birds have minds of their own and will do what they feel like doing.

When the cygnets get tired paddling behind their mother, she drops her tail like a drawbridge and up they scramble on to her back, glad of the rest and a lift home. They are indeed royal birds and behave accordingly.

Along the boardwalk, in a shallower part of the lough, we come across a sixteen-strong mallard duck family and friends outing. It's a mishmash of shapes and sizes. The youngest ducklings are only a few days old and are duly instructed by their mother to leave the grassy bank and have a paddle. Good as gold and seemingly undaunted by the height involved, one by one they scrabble over a stone and plop unceremoniously into the water.

Week by week, the ducklings will shed their fluffy feathers, which will be replaced by mottled plumage. Adults also go into this full eclipse after the breeding season, losing their old feathers to the extent that they are largely unable to fly. Left with brown feathers for camouflage, the male mallard now bears a very close resemblance to the female. Each species of duck goes through this process of moulting, and both male and female retain the speculum, the bright blue feathers on the side of their body, throughout. About three weeks after he has shed his feathers, the beautiful male mallard gets back his green head, white collar, maroon breast, grey body and black curly tail. Dot is at pains to point out that, despite not being a showstopper, the female mallard duck is beautiful in her own way.

If either of us could paint, we'd try to do justice to this uplifting tableau. Moorhens are swimming in the tall reed beds at the far side of the water. A pied wagtail is running along the top of a handrail, singing merrily. In the distance we hear the catchy refrain of willow warblers, blackcap, wren and chaffinch. Swallows are enjoying the tiny flies. The fast-flying swifts are high in the sky, shrieking, twisting and turning in perfect sequence. Hooded crows stalk the paths like sheriffs from a bygone era, ready to take action should the need arise. It may all be too much for Harry the Heron who has decided we must return another day for the pleasure of his company.

We have one final stop to make before lunch and as we drive through the towering gates of Portora Royal School on the Lough

Waterhens on Lough Erne
© Roy Crawford

Shore Road in Enniskillen, Dot is less than impressed at the suggestion of going back to school. But her initial cynicism gives way to the possibility of method in this madness.

One of the public schools founded by James I's Royal Charter in 1608, Portora was established ten years after the Royal Decree in 1618. It was initially based fifteen miles outside Enniskillen at Ballybalfour, before moving to Enniskillen in 1661. In 1778 this prestigious seat of learning moved to its final location on Portora Hill, Enniskillen, where the main building of the school was built. A mixture of boarders and day pupils attended Portora for much of its history, but it became a day school in the 1990s.

As well as Oscar Wilde, Samuel Beckett and hymnwriter and poet Henry Frances Lyte are among famous past pupils who attended what, at the time of its closure and amalgamation with Enniskillen Collegiate in 2016, was the oldest educational establishment in Northern Ireland.

Now Enniskillen Royal Grammar School, this elevated site overlooking woodlands is a mecca for long-tailed tits and blue tits, wrens, robins, dunnocks, goldcrest, chaffinch and blackbirds, all of which tend to opt for the outskirts of wooded landscapes. Chiffchaff, willow warblers and blackcap who have made the long journey from Africa are able to luxuriate in their made-to-measure nests in thick shrubs; jays, magpies, mistle and song thrush are happiest in the deeper parts of forests.

While the pupils at this illustrious institution look forward to a long, lazy summer, their fledgling, birding contemporaries have been enrolled in bird camp and are already busy learning vital lessons in how to fend for themselves and find natural food before the seasons change.

As we explore the grounds of the school, Dot comes to a stop beside a very large pine tree and cranes her neck to such an extent that I fear she'll do herself an injury. Before long she explains the reason for her contortions: ravens. Members of the crow family, these birds have a wonderful deep call and remarkable parental skills. Dot is transfixed as they holler back and forth to each other while herding their young in flight across the school's hallowed rooftops and then disappear into the comfort of their chosen tall tree. With an expansive wingspan, their size and diamond-shaped tail helps to distinguish ravens from rooks, crows and jackdaws.

By now, gulls are circling the playground in the hope of titbits from lunchtime treats. Even Dot would bestow gold stars on the lesser black-backed, herring and black-headed gulls for their time-telling skills. We don't need to check our watches to know that it's precisely the right moment to take our leave, find a picnic table and unwrap our sandwiches.

The beautiful island town of Enniskillen is blessed with myriad birdlife and as you dander along the shoreline from Castle Island to Portora Castle, it's refreshing to just tune in to nature. Graceful swans, energetic mallard ducks, cheeky moorhens, stern herons and, sometimes, a glimpse of the shy kingfisher. The uplifting sound of birdsong offers reassurance and hope, just like a bird that senses the dawn breaking and sings while it is still dark.

SELWYN JOHNSTON, HEADHUNTERS MUSEUM, ENNISKILLEN

Homebirds in Portstewart

*My love of seagulls began in the summer of 1978 when
Charlie the herring gull would visit the backyard of
my dad's cafe in Portstewart every day to be fed scraps
by hand from Mrs Bacon who worked there. We knew
it was him because he had a hole in his foot! He was
huge, always hungry and quite cheeky – but he liked
and trusted Mrs Bacon and me. And I loved him.*

NICOLE MORELLI

The last time Dot travelled from her seaside home in Bangor to mine
in Portstewart, the intermittent showers and persistent mizzle put
paid to any thoughts of ice cream or a dander on the prom. Another
visit was in the offing, so, by way of reparation, I double-checked the
weather forecast with my mother, who, as a keen dog walker, has tried
and tested ways and means of knowing when it's going to rain and
when you're safe enough for an hour or so.

Her method may not be an exact science but, in my experience,
it's foolproof. The theory is that, if you look left out of the front door,
towards the town, and the clouds are dark, then stay in. If you look
to the right, towards Coleraine, and the clouds are darkening, head
on out, though maybe not for too long. Either way, the weather gods
were smiling on us on the appointed day. Cecilia Daly had promised
sunshine, and she was right too.

I think it would be easier to teach a bird to talk than to find
a parking space on Portstewart promenade in summer, but against

the odds and armed with some local knowledge on where to park from her erstwhile birding companion, Dot managed it and we met at the Crescent, just opposite the town hall.

This historic building – two storeys in mellow redbrick with dressed stone surrounds and a hipped roof, to use the technical terms – was constructed in 1934 by the contractor F.B. McKee and designed by the architect Ben Cowser. The ground floor has, at different stages, contained both the library and the town clerk's office. The upper floor, accessed from the promenade, has tall perpendicular windows and, inside, an iron balcony.

The town hall holds special memories for me. When I was maybe eight or nine years of age, my parents sent me to elocution lessons with a gifted teacher called Margaret Watt, who taught youngsters from the town how to improve their diction and recite poetry, not to mention doing wonders for their confidence. Despite Dot's incredulity, I protest that I was a very shy child and that it was something of a miracle that I managed to stand on the stage of the town hall when I was nine years old and recite a poem called 'The Lonely Scarecrow'.

My recitation was performed as part of Coleraine Music Festival, which was part of the annual calendar of events, and included a number of competitions every summer in Portstewart. The place was packed with the proud mums and dads, grandparents, aunties, uncles, brothers and sisters of the well-turned-out youngsters from round the Triangle (the name locals use for the three north-coast towns of Portstewart, Portrush and Coleraine), all bidding to catch the attention of the judges, or at least remember the verses of the poem they were performing.

And so it was in 1974 that somehow I managed to do both and was presented with first prize and a cup for my efforts. My mini replica of the cup is still in the house and makes me smile every time I notice it. Sadly, the town hall is currently closed and in need of major repair work.

Beside the venue for my early and short-lived poetry career is

St Mary's Star of the Sea Catholic Church. This was built in 1916 and cost £6,000, which, during a primary school project, we youngsters were told would be the equivalent of millions in today's money. It's an imposing building in black basalt, with its yellow sandstone trim creating a dramatic contrast.

Overlooking the entire town of Portstewart, above the cliff path walk, is Dominican College, where I spent seven very happy years. In those days there were many teaching nuns and great young teachers who did their best to instil in their charges a degree of knowledge and, more importantly, a set of values that included doing your best and being kind.

The school, located on Strand Road, was formerly Rock Castle and was built in 1834 by Henry O'Hara, another of the founding fathers of the town. I remember reading somewhere that the writer William Makepeace Thackeray called the building 'a hideous new castle'. When O'Hara died in 1844, the castle was extended and a new seven-bay façade provided more bedrooms and reception rooms. Around the same time, the rubble basalt wall along the cliff edge was also built, perhaps as a famine relief project. As a youngster and oblivious to this poignant note, for me this three-storey building with its four corner turrets and gothic windows was like something out of a fairy tale.

In the late seventies I had a Saturday job in George Nicholl's VG shop on the Coleraine Road and through it I got to know the two local breadmen who made deliveries to the school: Walter, the Mother's Pride man and Norman, the Ormo man. On Wednesday and Friday afternoons, I'd watch keenly through the window of my Room 9 French class for Walter and Norman to drive their liveried vans through the big entrance gates. Quickly excusing myself from class, I would race down the corridor to head them off at the delivery door and, in an already agreed deal, promptly relieve them of any buns that were past their sell-by date.

The hard part was smuggling the buns back into class and

distributing them to the five people nearest me, away from the glare of the teacher. Necessity is the mother of invention and an oversized jumper designed to last for my entire seven-year tenure at school came in very handy.

There's only so much history a body can take and to avoid Dot's eyes glazing over, I hit the pause button on my nostalgic reminiscences to scout out the birds of the day, which turn out to be holidaymakers in the guise of Portstewart sand martins.

We walk along the lower prom, from the Witch's Hat at the Crescent steps towards the small harbour. Dot is striding out, warming to her subject and explaining enthusiastically that, all being well, there'll be a nesting colony of these fly-hoovering birds in the black basalt rock that forms part of the harbour wall. Naturally, she's right and I have to admit that in all my years of traipsing up and down the prom, climbing the harbour hill and fishing from the rocks as a child, I've failed to appreciate the existence and beauty of these tiny little birds.

This adds to Dot's enjoyment of the capers of the very busy sand martins. In flight, she says, the adults are easily identified by light brown upperparts, and a brown band across their white breast. They have a short tail and long, sharp wings designed for speed. From about mid-May, using their miniature feet they will dig a tunnel of about

Sand martin © Jonny Andrews

Sand martin nests
© Dot Blakely

60cm to 90cm in the sandbank, with an enlarged nesting chamber at the end of it. Both parents help with the care of the young, which can be as many as four or five. After nineteen days, a brood will take to the air, to consume as much food as possible before the long journey back to west Africa between August and September.

Dot loves to listen to the chatter, as she calls it, that happens between birds. In this case, at least twenty nesting sand martins are exchanging news as the young sit at the front of the nest hole, eagerly awaiting their lunch.

Others hurriedly fly past, towards the sandy cliffs, with a selection of flies in their large gape, ready to pass the food directly into the beaks of their young. It all happens at the speed of light. After the feeding, and in the blink of an eye the parents collect a wee parcel of poo from the babies that they'll dispose of at the first available random site. The moral of this story is, keep your mouth shut if you look up to watch these birds in action. This routine carries on for most of the day, until the young are full up. Bad weather, especially strong winds, can make the flies stay low, but that doesn't stop the sand martins hunting.

Sand martins are incredibly fast flying, able to move over grasses and reeds and around trees at breakneck speed. With a wide open beak, they hoover up the flies and store them at the back of their throat until the hunting is done and the feeding begins. In summer, they leave their wintering grounds in Africa as the temperatures rise, and come here to enjoy longer, cooler days, in a food-rich environment created by the climate in our northern location. So next time there's an intermittent, rainy-sunny summer, spare a thought for the thousands of flies this gives rise to and the happy sand martins who thrive here because of it.

Transfixed, we watch these compact birds coming and going and catching up on the news for quite a while. Small really is beautiful and very often can be found on your own doorstep.

Sand martins © Denis Chambers

As we head for an ice cream, my thoughts turn to the early settlers here, mostly fishermen and their families, back in the early nineteenth century, when the first purpose-built harbour was constructed in 1832. I imagine how tough their lives must have been and how very different Portstewart was then. While Thackeray wasn't a fan of Rock Castle when he visited in the 1830s, he was much more taken with the town, which, he said, 'had an air of comfort and neatness'. Perhaps the sand martins knew this all along.

We live and work in the heart of beautiful countryside. To listen to the song of birds from my window, watch the buzzards perched on the poles, or swooping into the fields so gracefully offers great comfort and peace. Nature is around us daily – we know we are so fortunate to be farmers and to be entrusted to look after our land for the next generation of farmers so they, too, can enjoy nature here at Broglasco.

LEONA KANE, FARMER

Gold Fever in Glenveagh

*I walk along the shores of the Lennon Valley in
County Donegal on a daily basis to be greeted by
a heron, a swan and many other delightful birds as
they watch in protection of their peaceful surroundings.
It makes me smile because I know I am safe
even on a misty morning.*

CIARA JOHNSTON, BBC PRODUCER

Dot made her first visit to Glenveagh National Park almost twenty years ago, with her Castle Espie birdwatching club. Given that this national park's reputation precedes it, there was only one species on everyone's mind on the journey to this five-star birding destination – the golden eagle.

The minibus was filled to capacity with thirty-two bright-eyed, fully rainproofed birding enthusiasts as it left the grounds of the Ulster Folk and Transport Museum in Cultra. A dull, dismal start to the day had made for an impressive array of water-resistant attire, from brightly coloured wellington boots and raincoats to shower-resistant, snugly-covered telescopes and binoculars. Firm believers that there is no such thing as bad weather, only the wrong clothing, the happy band of travellers remained optimistic, despite the unassailable reality, that the closer they got to Donegal, the heavier the rain also seemed to get.

At that time, Lorcan O'Toole was project manager of the Golden Eagle Trust at Glenveagh and part of the team charged with

managing the successful reintroduction of this exalted bird to the park. Glenveagh had been granted a special licence that allowed it to transport eagle eggs from Scotland to hatch at the park before eventual release into the wild landscape there. After an absence of over one hundred years, Glenveagh is rightly proud that the first golden eagles were released there in 2001.

Following an illuminating talk on the work that had been done, and the obligatory packed lunch of tea and sandwiches, the group headed for a walk around the lake. Donegal weather in summer can be prone to fits of pique and on this occasion was surpassing itself. Rain, rain, and more rain allowed the birders to test the limits of their wet gear. Moving as one large group, two and three abreast, an aerial view would have caught their resemblance to a slinking, rainbow-coloured, Chinese dragon.

After what Dot vividly remembers was a long, wet walk, the group arrived at the meeting-point opposite the waterfall at the other side of the lake. This is the optimum place in Glenveagh to catch a glimpse of golden eagles, as they favour the dizzy heights above the waterfall. Dot and her group were hoping against hope that a minor weather miracle would occur. Birds are exceedingly smart in regard to weather – they have to be to survive and outwit its twists and turns – and torrential rain generally means no birds will be seen or heard.

As if by magic, the monsoon abated and the clouds shrivelled away behind a determined ray of sunshine. As the sky slowly transformed from grey to cloudy blue, two golden eagles further illuminated the wild blue yonder, casting a hypnotic spell on the spectators. Dot's memory is that the eagles were playful in their movements and, like their awestruck, ground-based observers, just very glad of the dry air.

The display continued and, as the group watched in deferential silence, both golden eagles, in a final flourish, flew in tandem from the waterfall across the sheer expanse of the lake before rising high and disappearing over the mountain. No sooner had the eagles vanished than the rain returned with a vengeance. Nothing, however, could diminish the feeling of collective satisfaction in the assembled crowd. All that glitters may not be gold, but in the bird world, Dot and her club would beg to differ.

Wild bred golden eagle chick
© Golden Eagle Trust

One of six national parks in Ireland, Glenveagh is protected by EU and national law. It falls within both the Cloghernagore Bog and Glenveagh National Park Special Area of Conservation, and the Derryveagh and Glendowan Mountains Special Protected Area.

At 16,000 hectares, Glenveagh has a range of habitat types that includes uplands, woodlands, peatland and freshwater rivers and lakes. The age-old flora and fauna here have adapted well to the local climate and many of the species are unique to this part of the country. The diversity of habitats means that a wide range of birds live and thrive here.

The two highest mountains in County Donegal, Errigal and Slieve Snaght, are also enclosed within the park and, because it is an upland area, peregrine falcons are the predominant predators in the highest reaches of Glenveagh. They fly far and wide within these realms searching for food, choosing inaccessible south-facing cliff ledges to nest on for protection, warmth and light. Dot says it can be hard to pick them out, but that each year every suitable cliff will be occupied by a pair.

Other birds of prey that are spotted regularly in Glenveagh include merlins, small, fierce falcons that use surprise attacks to bring down songbirds; sparrowhawks, with their bright yellow eyes, broad wings, yellow legs and lethal talons; and kestrels, typically seen hovering, their pointed wings fully spread.

In the two decades since Dot's first trip to Glenveagh, she is happy to report that the golden eagles are still here and thriving. We're both hoping that on today's trip we'll get a chance to see them for ourselves. Our journey to the park proves that Dot is a very good co-pilot and navigator. She says it's years of practice and many car trips with Terry. As we make our way to Glenveagh, signs appear and disappear and the woman's voice on the sat nav chirps in occasionally, but not always helpfully. Dot and I maintain that sat nav's sister works at the International Airport at Aldergrove, directing luggage

Glenveagh National Park
© *Brid O'Donovan*

trolleys over the edge of the moving walkway.

The weather is typical for this time of year – cloudy with spits and spots of rain pebble-dashing the ground every so often. The sizeable car park is poor preparation for the staggering scene that reveals itself on leaving the visitors centre and heading down towards the bus stop. Dot's antennae are already tuned in and she says hello to the long-tailed tit families feeding on flies and spiders in the hedgerows and trees. In an instant, an alarm call spooks them. All seven babies go quiet and with the fully-grown birds trailing behind them, they swiftly disappear.

In between the raindrops, tiny midges emerge triumphantly from nowhere, hoping to sample our sandwiches and the impressive selection of pastries that Dot has thoughtfully packed. We don't give them the chance and hastily finish our stand-up picnic, return the bags to the car and make for the wonderland that awaits.

The birds seem to up the ante in an arena this size. Even as we walk through the woodland to the beautiful lake, wrens, robins, blackbirds, willow warblers and a song thrush are performing like seasoned professionals who will rise to any occasion in a venue like this. This vast outdoor auditorium ensures that their song carries high up into the mountains and can be heard in the valleys, glens and canyons that pepper this panoramic vista.

Along the edge of the lake, meadow pipits are calling in the rough grasses and skylarks return to their nests. As the rain continues to fall, it reminds Dot that, while absence may make the heart grow fonder, it can't make the sun shine, and we begin to wonder why we didn't catch the bus that trundled past on its way to one of many viewing points in Glenveagh.

For avid birders and first-time visitors to Glenveagh, the most prized sighting above all others is still that of the resplendent golden eagle. This time, we know the golden eagles have definitely landed, but they must be in a spot where they are dry and content as well as being well and truly hidden from view. Before we leave, we are

reliably informed that several eagles are seen regularly in the valleys of the park, secure in the knowledge that, from there, a tasty meal can be easily snatched.

Although we didn't catch a glimpse of this huge bird of prey on this occasion, we are both content and already making plans to return. Dot reiterates her conviction that it's not always about how many birds you see or hear, but about the beauty of the place and the sheer joy of just *being* that magical moments like this provide.

Perhaps because they provide a home for an abundance of bird species, Dot is an ardent fan of woodlands. Glenveagh, for example, can boast the wood warbler, an uncommon bird in Ireland but an annual visitor here, as well as the spotted flycatcher and chiffchaff who arrive from Africa in mid-May to exploit the seasonal increase in insect life here. There are also jays, treecreepers, chaffinch, song thrushes and robins. The main valley in the park is planted with conifer trees and this pinewood variety is ideal territory for crossbill, siskin, goldcrest and coal tit.

Lough Veagh near the castle in the park attracts waterfowl, including the eye-catching red-throated diver. Glenveagh has been a beneficiary of the healthy numbers of this bird that exist in Scotland and it now nests and breeds in small numbers here. They feed in the nearby coastal waters and their evocative high, wailing cry as they fly in from the sea to their nests is as much a part of summer mornings in the park as a cuppa at the wooden picnic tables.

There have been no sightings of the rare goosander duck in Glenveagh for several years, but there is talk of a collaboration with the Wicklow Mountains National Park in an effort to entice this elusive species back to Glenveagh.

The blanket bog and heath habitat that covers the vast majority of this stunning landscape is home to skylarks, red grouse, curlew and snipe. Dot agrees with the current guide that no bird captures the character of the uplands more evocatively than the golden plover. With a melancholy call, it opts to watch the passing throng from the safety of a stone or peat hummock. As a breeding bird, this beautiful plover is now quite rare in Ireland and is confined to the north and west of the country.

Dot is still buzzing and identifying bird after bird as we cast a final look back at this vast, rocky landscape. We are tiny specks, dwarfed by the sheer magnitude of Glenveagh. If there is a heaven on earth for birds, this surely must be it.

Birdwatching has been part of my life from the day a sparrow got into my house and landed on my cot, to my delight. Nature is something that I always feel at one with.

PAUL MCCULLOUGH

AUTUMN

Cormorants © Gary Gray

Brent geese on Strangford Lough with Scrabo Tower in the background © Michael Graham

A Gander at the Geese in Newtownards

As the days get colder, the Roe Estuary becomes a winter home for the Icelandic giants of the bird world – whooper swans. Gleaming white, in chevron flight, their honking calls and great whoosh of wings fills my heart with awe and joy.

HELEN MARK, BBC PRESENTER

Every year along the County Down coastline, thousands and thousands of pale-bellied brent geese flock to the shores of Strangford Lough. Dot has witnessed this incredible natural spectacle on many occasions and was eager for me to share in the excitement of this visual treat. While the Floodgates on the Portaferry Road in Newtownards may not sound like the most inspiring address, it's the best place in Northern Ireland to view up to twenty-five thousand brent geese that arrive here from Arctic Canada every August, September and October.

Immediately after the junction with the Old Shore Road, there is a car park on the right-hand side. En route to the Floodgates there are remarkable views of Scrabo Hill and Scrabo Tower. The car park leads to a walkway that stretches across the northern strand of Strangford Lough, bridging the sea defences that protect reclaimed lands to the south of Newtownards. The sea defences here were upgraded in 2000.

As you would expect, the embankment is a long, flat path. The story goes that a Dutch engineer was employed to build it in the second half of the seventeenth century in the hope that it would encourage a Dutch settlement at Newtownards. The current embankment dates from 1811 and was built by Lord Londonderry of Mount Stewart who reclaimed 200 acres of land at the head of Strangford Lough by building floodgates. He then turned the reclaimed land into arable farmland.

In the 1930s, Lord Londonderry donated 50 acres of his land to be developed into an airfield. Local farmers brought carts of stones to use as hardcore for the runways. There were two entrances to the airfield: one on the Portaferry Road, the other on the Comber Road. Some of the more enterprising farmers would bring their carts to the Portaferry Road entrance, get a ticket for their loads, leave by the other gate with the load covered and then go around the block for a second ticket, getting double the money for their entrepreneurial efforts.

When it comes to birds, this area is unique and of significant international importance. Up to seventy different species of birds arrive here in both summer and winter solely because of the food. The geese are joined by swans, wildfowl, terns, curlew, black-tailed godwit, bar-tailed godwit, oystercatchers and guillemots. If the food wasn't there, the birds wouldn't be either.

Towards the end of summer, there can be up to approximately 25,000 brent geese, over 2,000 shelduck and more than 200 whooper swans on a daily basis. It's a birdwatcher's paradise. The knots are especially worth looking out for – they lift together in their thousands, with distinctive silver and grey markings making it easier to pick out the variety of shapes they make as they fly overhead. The golden plover do the same, painting the sky with glittering gold and white streaks, all the while trying to avoid the high-flying lapwings with their large, broad wings.

On a perfect, autumnal September day, with little wind and clear skies, Dot has already scouted the perfect viewing point for us, about

Brent geese © Chris Henry

halfway along the crescent-shaped embankment. Armed with the binoculars that I made sure to bring, hoping to earn brownie points from Dot, I make my way to the appointed spot, and already there is a lot of activity along the shore and in the air.

Dot has the tripod up, telescope trained and her clicker at the ready. This clicker is a clever pocket-sized device that remains a bit of a mystery to me. It's the means by which officially approved 'counters' like Dot, help to record the numbers of pale-bellied geese that arrive here annually. The counts are done on a regular basis and the numbers reviewed each year in order to keep track of any fluctuations that might occur.

Dot is clicking away while looking through the telescope. She's excited. This is one of her favourite birding walks. She says that the best times to see the geese feeding are just as the tide is dropping or about an hour before high water. She reiterates that the reason these birds make the mammoth 3,000 mile trip to our shores is because of the readily available, high-quality meals on offer. Eel grass is the sought-after prize at the end of their arduous, exhausting journey from Canada.

Geese are highly sociable creatures too. The thousands of birds in the clear blue skies above us are making quite a noise. Dot says it's their way of saying, 'What about you? All right? How you doing? No, that's my spot,' – that kind of thing. A bit like us in many ways. Chat, chat, and more chat.

Very soon, all is quiet as the feeding frenzy begins. The tide has receded, exposing the all-important eel grass to the delight of the hungry brent and their broods. Now and again the adult geese lift their heads to check that it remains safe for the family – no predators – and that everyone is getting their share of the spoils.

We take time to savour and absorb this magnificent, natural spectacle. At full tide, there will also be pintail and shelduck, seemingly floating past in an almost trance-like state. The little egrets and herons mind their own business, unaware that there's anything special about what they're part of.

Peregrine falcons take much more of an interest in what they consider to be a very appetising menu of a wader or two for lunch. Dot is pragmatic about these natural predators – she doesn't like to see the kill, but they have young to feed too. These wonderful birds of prey are extremely agile, can accelerate towards their target in seconds and play an integral part in the balance of nature. She is at pains to add that all birds of prey are protected by law and should never be interfered with in any way.

Brent geese © Denis Chambers

On the other side of the coastal path, the waders are content to feed alongside stonechats, wrens, robins, meadow pipits, linnets and skylarks, who keep themselves to themselves in the neighbouring fields and hedgerows. Given that such a colourful and varied tableau is on offer, it's no wonder that this time of year at Strangford Lough is a highlight of Dot's birding calendar. At the other end of the lough, Island Hill car park, which looks towards Rough Island, provides another great vantage point for birders and nature lovers. Bring a flask, a few sandwiches and marvel at an impressive natural display that will draw you back again and again to the beautiful shores of Strangford Lough.

What The National Trust Says

The role that the National Trust plays in the management of Strangford Lough is crucial to the survival of brent geese. Strangford Lough Lead Ranger Hugh Thurgate points out that, through careful habitat management, the Trust maintains the mudflats and protects the eel grass population from invasive species, such as cord grass. If the eel grass can thrive, then the birds will continue to return and refuel on this high-protein food source.

At the moment, the brent geese are breeding well but this wasn't always the case. The population dipped to below ten thousand in the 1930s when eel grass declined significantly due to a wasting disease, proving the vulnerability of the brent geese as a species and its reliance on this food source.

Mount Stewart Ranger Toby Edwards explains that the National Trust also plays a key role in the management of the wildfowling activity in the area, working closely with the British Association for Shooting and Conservation and four local wildfowling clubs on a range of conservation projects. They create refuges for the birds, issue permits and patrol the shoreline during the shooting period between September and January.

Thanks to a successful tagging programme which began in 2003 in association with the Wildfowl & Wetlands Trust, the National Trust are well informed about the habits of brent geese, including their average ten to fifteen-year lifespan and their mating preferences. The birds pair for life and tend to breed alternative years. They are utterly loyal to each other and also maintain a strong family bond with their young.

'The birds that visit Strangford Lough are a unique ecological unit,' says Hugh, 'and thanks to the support of members and visitors, the National Trust is protecting their habitat for generations to come.'

Pale-bellied Brent Geese

There are two species of brent geese, dark and pale-bellied. The darker variety come from Northern Europe and Russia to winter in Scotland and England. But 80 per cent of the world's pale-bellied geese come to Strangford Lough in droves every August to October from the Canadian Arctic via the 2,700-metre-high Greenland ice cap. It's a colossal 3,000 mile journey that requires huge reserves of stamina and strength to complete in three months. The geese travel across Greenland, then stop off briefly in Iceland for a quick refuel. During this time, they sleep on the wing using a sophisticated in-built navigation system, just as their ancestors did time and again before them.

Small in stature, this distinctive goose is no more than 55-60cm in height. It has a small black head, with a black neck. Adults show a white neck ring, or patch as it is sometimes called, with plain grey upperparts and pale-bellied underparts. They fly in family groups, either in a V shape or in a loose group, and their white rumps allow them to see the goose in front. Like all geese, they are very good parents, and both male and female help to look after the young. They arrive at Strangford Lough in family groups when the young geese are about three months old. The young do not have the white neck ring or patch at this time and have white edges to their wings. While this coastal landscape is abundant in eel grass – the food of choice for the geese – it is also a rich picking ground for other small crustaceans and grass.

The geese settle at the top of Strangford Lough when they arrive but after a few weeks, as they exhaust the food supply, they move, down the lough, ending up in Dundrum Bay and even as far south as Dublin Bay, feeding constantly as they go. By February, they start to move back up to the top of Strangford Lough, getting together again in their pairs, before the big flight back home. Every year Dot wishes them luck and tells them she'll be waiting for them the next year.

The miracle of migratory birds is that they know no borders or boundaries and they travel where the seasons take them. None typify this more than swallows, house martins and swifts. They arrive in Ireland in the spring and herald the coming of summer – the combination of the swallow's song, the house martin's soft chirping and the swift's high-pitched scream provides us with a complete change to the pace of life. At the other end of the summer, the house martins congregate before leaving and we might see a couple of thousand at the front of the house and sitting on ledges. Simply magical.

Viscount Brookeborough

Looking for Sanderlings in Magilligan

How lovely to wake up on a spring morning and to have the privilege of listening to the wonderful dawn chorus just outside my window. Blackbirds, robins and thrushes are quickly joined by wrens and finches – and in Portstewart, even the odd seagull. Together they produce a joyous symphony, which is delightful, uplifting and comforting. It's also a reminder of the great beauty and simple pleasures that surround us.

VIVIEN LEIGHTON

When I was a youngster, one of my favourite Sunday runs was to my granny's homeplace in Magilligan on the shores of Lough Foyle. At eight or nine years of age, I suspect the full impact of the natural beauty of the place might have been a bit lost on me. These days, quite the reverse is the case. It's one of the joys of my life to drive along the stunning coastal road from Downhill to Limavady, soaking up the sheer artistry of this enchanting landscape. On one side is the historic nineteenth-century railway line, cleverly positioned at the foot of the towering, grassy, rock-strewn cliffs with their head-turning waterfalls. On the other, the seven-mile-long beach that makes Benone Strand one of the longest in Northern Ireland.

Magilligan gets its name from 'MacGilligans country', which

formed a major part of the barony of Keenaght. It's a peninsula in the north-west part of County Derry, at the entrance to Lough Foyle, and served as the base line for triangulation for the mapping of Ireland in the nineteenth century. Colonel Thomas Colby chose it due to the flatness of the countryside and its proximity to Scotland which, along with the rest of Britain, had already been accurately mapped.

In the days when radio recordings were done using a heavy, reel-to-reel recorder, I hauled this unwieldy contraption along with myself into the rear seat of a sleek glider, behind the pilot, and prepared for take-off from Magilligan's flat, fertile fields, beneath Binevenagh mountain.

That flight was thirty years ago and it has lived long in my memory. For two reasons. First, because my dad was right about the scenic panorama and second because the experience of gliding through the thermals and relying entirely on the summer breeze that day made me wonder if birds in flight also make use of these natural navigational tools.

My father, Maurice, has a special place in his heart for this entire area. As a boy, he spent his summer holidays on his grandparents' small farm in Magilligan. To him it was a magical place, self-contained in every respect and symbolising now a way of life that has gone forever. In his book, *Back Through the Fields*, he describes the thatched cottage where his grandparents lived; no electricity, no running water, but all the home comforts they needed and always a welcome on the mat.

They kept a few chickens and a couple of cows, so there was no shortage of milk or eggs. One of young Maurice's jobs included helping with breakfast: 'I remember many a morning being sent down to the henhouse, where there were rows of neat boxes filled with straw for the nesting hens, to gather a few eggs for breakfast, and often I had to persuade a reluctant hen to move so that I could claim the trophy. I could feel the eggs warm in the palm of my hand as I lifted them out.'

My father told me these stories time and again over the years, on those occasions when we walked back through the fields that enveloped his childhood, leaving cherished memories that have sustained him throughout his life.

So, when Dot mentioned that autumn and winter are good times to see stonechats, reed buntings, linnets, wrens, robins and skylarks and then added that Magilligan Point would be the best place to go, there was more than a spring in my step on a crisp, cold November morning.

Dot thinks nothing of making a two-hour journey in search of her feathered friends. This particular trip from Bangor to the north-west was also a good excuse for her to make a quick stop at Toome and a site near the village that supports thousands of water birds in the autumn. On this chilly but dry day, she was delighted to see that hundreds of beautiful whooper swans were contentedly roaming the fields near the A6.

When we get to Magilligan Point, the prospect of what we might see has Dot excited. As we walk through the sandhills, she says that in the summer the dunes are full of different bugs, moths and butterflies and I point towards where my great-grandparents thatched cottage used to be, smiling at the notion that, like Dot, they too would have been on first-name terms with the wildlife and birds.

Empty cocoon cases from hatched burnet moths festoon the long wild plant stems and there are mouse holes in the sandbanks. On the soft, sandy beach, just beside the Martello tower, we start looking for sanderlings, small black and white or brown and white waders. Dot reports that they often look as if they're engaged in a comical game of tag: they run into the tide in search of tiny insects, then speedily run back out to avoid getting their feet wet, feeding constantly while on the move. One minute they're chasing the waves, the next, it's the reverse, and the waves are on their tails. Today, however, the Magilligan sanderlings are a no-show.

Magilligan Point is also somewhere that snow buntings can be

seen. They are passerine birds, sometimes known as perching or song birds, and have three toes that point forward and one that points back to help with perching. But today they are also noticeable by their absence. However, the curlews, redshanks and ringed plover are in fine form, enjoying a brunch of flies, marine lugworms, crustaceans and molluscs, all freely available along the water's edge.

Shags and cormorants are roosting side by side on a large basalt rock out in the water, their wings fully extended. These birds are similar in looks, though the cormorant is a heavier bird and sits low in the water. It has a wedge-shaped angular-looking head and bulky bill. Shags are also coastal birds, but smaller than cormorants, with a slender body, a long, slim bill, dazzling emerald eyes and a short crest.

Dot is nothing if not vigilant and is now extolling the virtues of the fishing gannets, who prefer to fly high and far out to dive in the deeper parts of the sea, and the beautiful eider ducks. All of a sudden, Dot goes very quiet – experience has taught me not to speak when this happens. She has one particular gannet in her sights. It's been hanging high beneath the clouds, head pointed down, large black-tipped white wings swept back into a spear-like tip, ready to dive into the deep water. The plunge-point has been expertly identified and the launch happens at rocket-like speed, the winged angler emerging

Snow bunting © Chris Henry

triumphant, moments later, having made short work of his catch. All this feasting was making us hungry. But there was something else we wanted to investigate before we stopped for lunch.

The Martello tower at Magilligan Point is particularly well preserved. It was built around 1812, during the Napoleonic Wars, to guard against possible invasion. A well-known landmark, it marks the entrance to Lough Foyle. In total, seventy-four Martello towers were built in Ireland, forty of which still exist.

The towers were constructed at strategic points all around the coast and designed to fire on any invading fleet or to withstand lengthy sieges. Experts say that this tower marks the end of a long tradition in Ireland of erecting defensive buildings stretching back over three thousand years to Bronze Age forts.

As Dot and I get closer to the tower, feeling smaller with every step, we begin to get a better grasp of its scale. It's a curiosity for visitors and Discover Northern Ireland helpfully provides useful information on its website:

The walls are over 9ft thick and built of imported stone. There are three floors. The top floor housed a twenty-four pound cannon gun able to swivel and shoot in any direction. There was a small furnace to heat the gunpowder so it would be able to set wooden ships on fire. The middle floor was the living quarters for one officer and twelve men. A cellar below was accessed by a spiral staircase. There is a water well and storage rooms for munitions and food. Originally the entrance to the tower would have been via a wooden ladder but that has been replaced by an iron staircase.

It's a strange feeling to be standing right beside this man-made historic structure in such a natural landscape. The tower is located within Magilligan Point Nature Reserve at the edge of Northern Ireland's largest sand-dune system. The ever-changing tides and storms mean that the profile of the beach, the dunes, and the shape of the 'Point' itself, are also always in flux.

The mature or 'grey dunes' have well-established populations of mosses, lichens, grasses, herbs and higher flowering plants, providing a good nectar source for bees, butterflies and moth species. The rare scarce crimson and gold moth, which is found in only two places in the UK, has been recorded here. Secure in the knowledge that if anyone asks about the Martello tower at Magilligan, we'll be fit to answer, we head for a lunch that doesn't include flies or spiders.

We love birdwatching, learning to identify the birds by sight and sound. We have even introduced our grandson to it.

Cheryl Harbinson

© Aidan McCann

The **gannet** is the UK's largest seabird, with a wingspan of up to 1.8m. It has white plumage, black wing tips and a buff-coloured head and nape. The bill is powerful and strong, designed for fishing and diving from heights of up to 30m. Gannets have a reputation for being greedy but studies have found that this is inaccurate – they don't steal their rivals' food or have an unnaturally large appetite.

© Denis Chambers

At up to 90cm in size, **cormorants** are large, long-necked seabirds. Their stance is penguin-like, with short legs well back on their dark body, webbed feet and a long, strong, yellow hooked bill that helps them to swim fast and low in the water to catch fish. Adults have white cheeks and a white patch on the thigh. Cormorants can also be found inland on lakes and rivers.

The **shag** can be up to 76cm tall and is remarkably similar in body shape to the cormorant. They are dark green in colour, with a fine yellow bill. Adults have a short crest. After fishing, they can often be seen sitting on rocks drying off outstretched wings, in much the same way as a cormorant does.

© Chris Henry

A fully-grown **eider duck** can be 58cm. It's our largest diving duck and can reach a depth of 20m to feed on shellfish. The males have low sloping foreheads, a black cap and belly, green nape and bill, with a mostly white body and pink chest. Females are the same size and shape, but more mottled brown in colour for camouflage when they nest. They often roost in colonies on offshore islands, coastlands or rivers and can be found in rough seas in large groups or resting and feeding on molluscs on offshore rocks around the coast. Numbers here in Northern Ireland increase in winter with many eider ducks arriving from Northern Europe.

© Paul McCullough

Selling Your Garden to Birds

Birds need to know they are safe in a garden. Dot believes the fewer cats around the better for our instinctively anxious friends. She also thinks it's a good idea for keen birdwatchers to think of themselves in autumn and winter as estate agents.

In a similar way to making a house sale-ready, this is the time to sell your garden as a place to visit. Ivy on walls, thick hedgerows and maybe a bramble corner with old logs for bugs and insects is a good start. With any luck, a hedgehog might overwinter here as well. Dot knows from experience that children love getting their hands dirty and especially enjoy constructing bug hotels. A pond is a pleasing feature in any outdoor space. Dot believes that, no matter the size, a water feature is also a very handy thirst-quencher for the birds.

Old, thick ivy makes a snug home for spiders and flies. Dot counts herself fortunate to have an ivy wall at the back of the house that her trusty gardener Terry beautifies every spring time. Dunnocks and blackbirds nest here. It is sheer bliss for Dot and Terry to sit and watch their comings and goings and hear the young hungrily shouting for lunch. A bit like me with dogs and cats and any animals I come across, Dot chats away to her garden birds. She says hello from a distance, reassures them that everything is okay and reminds them that she definitely will not be looking into their nests.

The magpies are also well aware of Dot's regular forays into the garden and are content in her company too. She believes the most trusting bird is the blue tit and, therefore, the easiest bird to encourage to nest in the garden. The key thing here is that the nest box is positioned in the right place, ideally north-east facing and high up on a tree that will provide shelter from sun and rain. The blue tit will use the tree to get into the box. The entrance hole should be 25mm in diameter and 3mm larger for the great tit.

Thick hedgerows are firm favourites with house sparrows. They live in family groups and the constant chatter among them is wonderful to listen to. Naturally it's important to know if you have anything nesting before you cut or trim the hedgerow. Look carefully for signs of poo on the leaves and, more importantly, listen intently for sparrows tweeting, chirping and calling.

The more natural the habitat you can create, the better. In essence, the more greenfly, ants, spiders and worms you have, the more chance there is that a bird will nest in your garden.

In warmer weather, Dot delights in sitting outdoors, watching the tiny flies inadvertently becoming fast food for the hungry birds – hamburgers for birds she calls them. She could watch the birds do this for hours on end – catching lunch or dinner by flying up at them or picking them off the bushes. Biodiversity in action.

Given the chance, starlings might nest in roofs. Should this happen, by law you must wait until they have left their chosen site before blocking the entrance. A good idea is to put up your own starling nest box which they may well try out the next year.

On occasion, a sparrowhawk will spy out, hunt and kill a garden bird. This can happen at any stage in the year. However brutal this behaviour might seem, Dot thinks of it as part of the natural cycle of life. They also have families to feed, are instinctively hunters and shouldn't be disturbed in the course of their daily toil.

In general, birds are not high maintenance. They require plenty of food and shelter from rain or sunshine. In Dot's experience, once they get acquainted with us, they're also partial to a jabber. She has learned the language of birds through trial and error over many years and recommends it thoroughly as a way to enrich our lives.

A Murmuration in Belfast

Watching a huge group of starlings in full, fantastic flight, perfectly in harmony – a murmuration – is an amazing sight to behold. Just how these birds manage to maintain such a high level of graceful synchronisation while twisting and turning and weaving in all directions really is awe-inspiring. Perhaps one day someone will be moved to write a symphony based around their beautiful aerial dance. 'Flight of the Starlings' has a nice ring to it.

Maurice McAleese

The first day of June 1889 was a red-letter day in Belfast. Queen Victoria's grandson, Prince Albert Victor, was arriving in the city to lay a foundation stone on the bridge across the River Lagan that was to be named after him. Two arches of the previous bridge had suddenly collapsed in 1886, and in 1889 the Belfast Corporation had agreed to undertake the work required to restore the structure. Completed a year later, in 1890, the new bridge had three arches and was a welcome and impressive replacement of the temporary wooden bridge near the city centre that linked East Bridge Street and the Albert Bridge Road.

In the reports of the royal visit at the time, there is no mention of thousands of starlings filling the sky above the imposing new feat of engineering. Nor do I remember my granny, a proud Belfast woman, ever mentioning this now much-talked-about phenomenon.

As a child, I loved going to stay with my Belfast granny. From her house on the Lisburn Road, it was no distance to the city centre where we often spent a morning or afternoon dandering around the shops. We'd have lunch or a cup of tea and a pastry in one of the upmarket eateries near City Hall or on Royal Avenue and then get the bus back to the stop at the top of Surrey Street.

For an eleven-year-old, those days out with my granny in the city felt elegant and grown-up. Some days we would walk to the museum near Botanic Gardens and visit the gardens when the weather was nice. This was my first experience of 'culture' and instilled in me not only a love for the outdoors and history, but also a deep-rooted lifelong affection for Belfast.

Long after those carefree, childhood days, when granny had moved to Portstewart and I had just passed my driving test, I tried to return the favour and took her for days out round the Triangle. Despite her best efforts, I got the impression that she still longed for the city streets that she knew so well. I often think of her on trips to the city that include a dander along the Lisburn Road and, now and again, I make a detour and head for Surrey Street. She was definitely right about one thing – at times it's a lot colder in Portstewart than it is in Belfast.

Either way, I don't have to be asked twice to spend time in the city. And when Dot said we must go and see the starlings at the Albert Bridge, I didn't quite understand what she was referring to. I soon found out that vast numbers of starlings swirling above the bridge has become an unmissable autumnal spectacle.

These days Belfast is harder to navigate than when my granny and I were getting the bus from the City Hall. It's easy to find yourself in the wrong traffic lane and at the wrong bridge. Which is what happened to Dot as I kept a careful eye out for her from my vantage point below the Albert Bridge, and within sight of the ten-metre-long *Salmon of Knowledge* ceramic sculpture, just as dusk was falling.

Since what we were there to witness happens in the minutes it takes for dusk to turn to darkness, there was still plenty of time. Once in position and content, Dot explained that what the starlings do is called a murmuration. Standing underneath the bridge as the cars thunder along above us, I remembered that I'd heard that term before on a quiz show. And then wondered if 'murder' really was the collective name for crows. But for the moment, it was all about the starlings and the bird whisperer had all the answers.

In autumn and winter, large numbers of starlings migrate to the UK from Northern Europe for the milder temperatures and easier access to food. More and more of the birds will flock together between

*A murmuration of starlings over
Belfast's Albert Bridge © Paul McCullough*

October and November, and the number of starlings in a roost can
swell to around 100,000 in some places. Early evening, just before
dusk, is the best time to see them right across the country. No special
equipment is required as it's all visible to the naked eye. You just
need to look up.

In Belfast, the murmuration starts at around four o'clock, as the
light begins to fade, and lasts until it's dark, when the birds go to
roost underneath the bridge for the night. It's almost surreal. Like
a beautifully choreographed evening dance, the starlings turn and
twist, creating black shadows and patterns against the pale grey sky.

Resident and visiting starlings mix seamlessly in this virtuoso display, and Dot says the chat will be about where they've been all day, where the best food is and where they're headed to the next day. As the numbers increase to tens of thousands, it is nothing short of a miracle that there are no collisions among the birds or indeed with the bridge itself. The noise of the wingbeats as the starlings fly past is deafening. They move together at great speed, especially if they are being hunted by a peregrine falcon, the fastest raptor in the skies; they know well that there's safety in speed.

The general ornithological consensus is that starlings are every bit as intelligent as other, more common, pet bird species and can learn to talk. European starlings are accomplished mimics, often copying songs or the sounds of other birds and animals – such as frogs, goats and cats – and even mechanical noises. According to some experts, starlings can learn to talk better than parrots.

Dot feels that the starling's reputation as a garden bully is unfair and that people should give them a second look. They are skilled at defending themselves and often provide protection for other birds too. They also have an excellent strategy for dealing with potential predators. One starling will always be on guard, watching for birds of prey, such as sparrowhawks. Any sightings will prompt it to sound an alarm call, which the other starlings and smaller garden birds will heed and respond to immediately. The starlings will then lift up high and, as a group, attack the sparrowhawk, who they hope will think twice before repeating the offence. By then, the other small birds will have disappeared into the nearest hedgerows for safety. Starlings are indeed smarter than the average bird.

A small group of starlings live near Dot and she has observed that, in July and August, as the family grows, they will get together with other small, local families in preparation for the huge, sellout, star-spangled murmuration later in the year.

Watching this evening's murmuration only seems to reinforce Dot's firm belief that starlings are clever birds – they'd have to be to orchestrate these evening performances. Precise logistics on such a scale requires planning and communication, with a strong focus on the pecking order: who goes under the bridge first, who's less scared of a bird of prey, and who will roost first. Once this is all worked out, the swirling shadows thin out, the birds disappear, and the chatter gives way to a tranquil silence. For them, it's time for sleep. For us, it's eyes back down to earth and, later, a soft cushion for our strained necks.

© Paul McCullough

Starlings are most commonly seen in gardens and parks. They are very family-orientated and, at 22cm, a bit smaller than a blackbird. Adults have the most stunning purple-green gloss colours and a sharp bill for digging out worms and insects. They like to nest in holes in trees and under roof tiles. They also have a penchant for tumultuous city centres and often nest in large numbers under bridges. Their nightly dusk-to-dark performance is a spectacle known as a murmuration. They have an extensive song repertoire that contains many different notes, and they can mimic car horns, alarms, phones and other electronic devices that emit short sharp sounds.

I live in a first-floor flat and have feeders on my balcony. I get enormous pleasure from watching the sparrows, robins and tits that visit daily.

VAL MARSHALL

Nest Boxes
Dot's Dos and Don'ts

Birds will only use nest boxes if they want to, if they feel safe and if they can get natural food like greenflies or caterpillars close by. Dot has drawn up a handy list of what works and what doesn't when it comes to building and placing nest boxes.

✖ Don't cut hard into ivy, hedgerows or thick bushes after 1 March.

✖ Don't put a nest box up where it will get drenched by the rain.

✖ Don't put a nest box up where it will get the full glare of the sun.

✖ Don't put a nest box up where a cat or person can get to it.

✖ Don't put too many boxes close together as this can lead to fighting and stress among the smaller birds.

✖ Don't look into your box. Birds will often abandon the nest if they are disturbed.

✖ Don't put anything in the box.

✖ Don't put a feeder close to the box – feeders should not be needed in summer.

✖ Don't expect your birds to fly back and forward across an open space carrying food to the box.

✓ Do put your nest box near the cover provided by a tree or ivy.

✓ Do listen to the calls from your nesting birds – if you are too close, the birds will let you know, so listen for an alarm call.

✓ Do let your bird see you in the garden to let them know that you are around but won't get too close.

✓ Do chat to your birds. It lets them know you are there.

✓ Do keep cats, dogs and youngsters away, especially when the young are about to fledge – this is a very vulnerable time for the birds.

✓ Do enjoy this wonderful time, safe in the knowledge that you are playing your part in improving the quality of life for your home birds.

Blue tits and coal tits are the most common bird to use a nest box. The entrance hole should be 25mm. For great tits it should be slightly bigger at 28mm, and for sparrows, 32mm.

Nesting season can start from the end of March, so put the nest box up in autumn or early spring, ideally north to north-east facing.

House sparrows don't usually use nest boxes as they prefer to nest in colonies. Sometimes, they will take up residence in a communal box.

Waders in Whitehead

The Greeks believed that the heron was a messenger of the gods. When the herons call from their nests in the Dark Wood in Garvagh Forest everything falls silent; their call seems primordial, from another land and time. They lumber off their nests and the sky above the Norway spruces darkens a little with their wingspan.

KARIN EYBEN

Both Dot and I consider ourselves very lucky to have grown up on beautiful parts of the coastline in Northern Ireland. Bangor in County Down and Portstewart in County Derry are hard to beat when it comes to seaside towns. Since she was knee-high to a long-legged heron, Dot has explored the places in and around her home town in search of the bird life that intrigued her. For as long as I can remember I have cherished that I live in Portstewart and don't have to survive on two-week rations of the seaside from one summer to the next.

There is one place, though, where we both could happily spend our holidays. Brimming with charm and style, Whitehead is quintessentially Victorian in style and famous for the colourful, tall, elegant houses on its seafront. Only twenty miles from Belfast, and halfway between Larne and Carrickfergus, Whitehead has been a popular holiday destination for city dwellers here since the arrival of the railway in the nineteenth century, and now attracts an increasing number of international visitors. Once when I was there, I met a Danish woman from Copenhagen who was so smitten with the place that she upped sticks and made Whitehead her permanent home.

Maybe it was Muldersleigh Hill that caught her imagination. It's 131 metres high and stands above Whitehead like a conscientious sentry. The views from its summit – of the Mournes, the Antrim Coast, and, on a clear day, Scotland – are striking. The village sits snugly at the foot of this hill, in a small bay between the limestone cliffs of Whitehead and the volcanic cliff of Blackhead. Blackhead Lighthouse is an important beacon and signifies the entrance to Belfast Lough.

As well as charm, Whitehead has quirks. There are no roads with 'Street' in their name, which very quickly gave rise to the nickname 'The Town With No Streets'. Whitehead is also home to the Railway Preservation Society of Ireland, has a fully conserved railway station and is the starting point for the jaw-dropping Gobbins cliff path experience. The town also had an aerodrome, which housed two airships during the First World War.

In the late nineteenth century, when train travel reigned supreme, Whitehead was a railway excursion town. The station opened in May 1863, and in 1907 a dedicated excursion platform was added.

Berkeley Deane Wise was the visionary Irish railway engineer who took tourism to a new level in Northern Ireland. Originally from Wexford, he believed that creating new paid-for attractions would encourage people to use the train to get away from the humdrum of everyday life. Whitehead was one of the places that he chose to develop as a tourist destination, designing and building a bandstand, ladies and gents bathing boxes, a 'children's corner', a slipway and a pavilion with five hundred seats.

In 1892, Wise was also largely responsible for the Blackhead Path, stretching along the coast between Whitehead and the lighthouse at Blackhead. Along the route there were a number of bridges and a tunnel. Perhaps this was an early prototype for his grand ambition

Black guillemot © Paul Hunter

to build and design the Gobbins path on the sheer cliffs just a few miles away.

No doubt Berkeley Wise and the Victorians would be pleased and proud that in 2012, in keeping with what they started, Northern Ireland's only Jubilee Wood was planted at Whitehead to celebrate the Diamond Jubilee of HRH Queen Elizabeth II.

Had it been brighter, calmer and less rain-sodden the day we went to Whitehead, Dot could probably have waved at the fulmars and black guillemots on the Copeland Islands and at her friends in Bangor from our rendezvous-point beside Blackhead Lighthouse on the northern shores of Belfast Lough.

Despite the wind doing its level best to whip up a storm, undeterred and with my trusty golf umbrella up, we made for a buffer and the relative shelter offered by an unsuspecting camper van. Neither of us twigged that there were in fact people inside enjoying a cuppa and observing the worsening weather from the right side of the window. Now they had extra entertainment in the form of two strange women trying to get to grips with an oversized brolly, a tape recorder and a pair of binoculars.

Blissfully unaware and determined to catch a glimpse of some kind of bird activity, we persevered. Dot is not easily put off. Kitted out top-to-tail in wet gear with a matching peaked cap guaranteed to keep her dry, to my surprise, she announces that the tide is perfect. Keeping company with an optimist is infectious and, rather than ask why, I nod in agreement, not having the faintest idea what Dot is talking about, but certain that the science bit is about to be divulged. Sure enough, she tells me that when the tide is on the turn, the stony, muddy beach is laid bare, which means the freshly revealed rocks will offer copious amounts of seaweed, just what the covetous waders have been waiting for. Of course. Perfect.

And the waders are not the only ones with their eyes on the prize. First to fly in with its distinctive high-pitched call is the redshank. In fact, the extended family are all here too. One after another they land and start feeding hungrily on small marine invertebrates. As the tide reveals more soft mud, oystercatchers, dunlin and curlew have all caught the brisk lough-shore winds and show up out of nowhere, eager to share the spoils.

As the curlew is the largest European wading bird, it has the confidence to move out across the mud, and with its long, down-curved bill can expertly get to the lugworms underground. Simultaneously, like skilled chefs shucking an oyster, the black and white oystercatchers use their long, chisel-like, orange bills to make short work of the hard-shelled mussels and cockles.

Loose groups of the medium-sized dunlin, with their slightly thicker, down-curved bill, probe for molluscs and crustaceans along the water's edge. Dot's favourite waders are turnstones. If they were tins of varnish, they'd do exactly what it says on the tin. In another engineering triumph, they operate in precisely the way they are designed to, constantly turning stones to expose sandhoppers, and flipping over seaweed, seeking flies and small, shoreline creatures. It's a seamless operation. Each bird can find what they want to eat

Waders © Juliet Fleming

because their bills are different shapes and sizes.

It takes knowledge and a skilled eye to decipher and effortlessly explain the behaviour of large groups of bird species all in action at the same time. For as long as I have known her, Dot wears this proficiency very lightly. Her mission in life is to encourage her students and open up the wonderful world of birding in as accessible a way as possible. This she does with aplomb.

The scene before us is mesmerising, and the unfolding story that it presents is more than enough to sideline the inclement weather. Out on the water my faithful, ever-hopeful seagull friends wait for titbits from the fishing cormorants and eider ducks. Dot says that in the breeding season the cliffs here will have fulmars, gulls, black guillemots and ravens.

Thousands of waders overwinter around our coastlines, along with rock pipits, starlings, linnets and sparrows who also feed in the seaweed. But they must eat quickly and move away fast to the safety of long grasses or reeds as peregrine falcons very probably live close by and are also on the lookout for a good lunch.

Suddenly the camper van door opens. We say hello, explain ourselves and thank our bemused windbreakers. Dot's husband Terry is a mechanical genius and we wonder if he could fashion a wind and waterproof jalopy for all his bird women's travelling needs. We could road test it on our next visit to Whitehead.

© Paul Hunter

Common guillemots (34cm) are members of the auk family and, along with razorbill and black guillemots, breed along some of our coastal cliffs. In summer, the plumage is completely dark except for a white wing-patch, red legs and a red gape. In winter, the feathers and upperparts have black and white bars, while the head and underparts are pure white. The white wing-patch and red legs are still present and this helps with identification. Like most auks, black guillemots stand very straight and upright as the legs are far back in the body. This allows for efficient swimming and a rapid take-off, aided by fast beats of their short wings. They are excellent divers and do this routinely to catch fish.

Silence is golden, unless broken by birdsong. Even the raucous voice of the crow, which should be oiled, has a golden key capable of chasing plundering cats.

DOREEN MCBRIDE

Once Upon a Time in the Glens

In the early morning before sunrise, the blackbird singing in my garden is always the first bird I hear. What a singer and what a song: 'Today is a good day and all is going to be well!'

KIERAN MCALEESE, MUSICIAN

Once upon a time, there was a woman who was a very good storyteller. She lived in Glenballyeamon, one of the nine Glens of Antrim. People came from far and wide to hear her stories and her name was known all over the country and well beyond these shores, in lands far, far away.

If I was writing a story about Liz Weir MBE, this might well be how I'd begin. She is revered locally and around the world for her inimitable ability to engage an audience with age-old tales or original fables that she has authored. In 2019, she was honoured by Queen Elizabeth II for her services to storytelling.

A barn adjacent to her cottage in Glenballyeamon was converted for use as a venue for regular storytelling sessions. During the pandemic lockdown, when it wasn't possible to meet, Liz and her barn went digital and her virtual evenings regularly attracted hundreds of keen listeners and tellers from around the globe.

When I think of the Glens of Antrim, this doyenne of storytellers immediately springs to mind. She moved here from Ballymena in 1999 and Glenballyeamon has been home ever since. If Liz is not writing and performing herself, she is teaching and encouraging others in the ways of this ancient, oral tradition. Many of her stories feature birds, and I know she approves of Dot's respect and love for these creatures.

The nine glens stretch from the Antrim plateau to the coast road between Larne and Ballycastle. An area of Outstanding Natural Beauty and an international tourist attraction, this otherworldly landscape featured many times in the hit HBO television series *Game of Thrones.*

Once, on a trip to Glenravel (the unofficial tenth glen), a woman talked me through the meaning of each of the glen names: Glenarm is valley of the army; Glencloy, valley of the dykes; Glenariff is valley of the lough; Liz's glen, Glenballyeamon, is Edwardstown glen; Glenaan, valley of the little fords; Glendun means brown valley; Glenshesk, valley of the sedge; Glencorp, valley of the dead; and Glentaisie is named after Taisie, princess of Rathlin.

This is a centuries-old landscape and there is no shortage of evidence of Neolithic communities throughout the glens. Megalithic tombs have been uncovered in the uplands of Glencloy, which archaeologists regard as proof of farming communities living here and along the Dun, Dall, Glenshesk and Glenariff rivers, as both environments provided vital food for sustenance and flint for heat and tools.

Experts also believe that there were Neolithic tool production sites at Glenarm and in parts of County Antrim, including Carnlough, Templepatrick, Lyles Hill and Donegore Hill. At 'Madman's Window' near Glenarm, a treasure trove of stone-axe roughouts was found, together with chipping floors, pottery, scrapers and arrowheads. In Carnlough, at Bay Farm, a Neolithic site was discovered near marshland and archaeologists also found charcoal, debris, postholes, axes and flint cores.

Dot and I have made several trips to Glenarm. Often we go to the forest where dippers and grey wagtails can be found in pairs along sections of the river. These old woodlands also have a healthy red squirrel population, thanks in no small way to the good work of the Glens of Antrim Red Squirrel Group. The ancient trees attract

a variety of woodland birds, including the entire tit family, finches, thrushes, blackcaps, goldcrests, treecreepers, nesting buzzards, herons and, in summer, singing blackcap, chiffchaff and willow warbler.

This time, Dot suggests that we meet in the car park beside the shingle beach in the village, the favoured territory of one of our smallest waders, the ringed plover.

In advance of my arrival, Dot has been on a reconnaissance mission which has yielded a moment to cherish. Walking to the mouth of the little river that runs through the village to exchange pleasantries with the common gulls and mallard, out of nowhere a tiny flash of blue streaks past. The kingfisher punches way above its weight as far as dramatic entrances and exits are concerned. His unnoticed resting place had been on a fence post, close to the river bank, not far from the sea.

Dot says that where there are rivers or lakes there will, in all probability, be kingfishers. These brightly coloured birds have an uncanny knack of stealing the show, not just because of their dazzling coat of many colours but also because of their ability to appear in an instant, as if by magic, and then disappear again just as quickly. On the day we visit, Dot's Glenarm star of the show does exactly that, absconding rapidly under the bridge and fluttering away up river.

We turn our attention to the chorus line of ringed plovers as they

Ringed plover © Paul Hunter

prepare their well-rehearsed moves for today's performance.

If they were in a stage show, their costumes would resemble brown and grey tuxedo jackets over crisp white shirts, with striking black and white facial masks. All in all, they cut quite a dash, despite being upstaged earlier by the unexpected arrival of the flamboyant Mr Kingfisher.

Feeding on flies, spiders, marine worms, crustaceans and molluscs, the plovers seem insatiable. They are seasoned troupers and a sizeable cast has assembled on the sandy stage. Keeping time with the tide, they walk quickly, stop and pat the sand to uncover this morning's delicacy, all in perfect harmony, over and over again: run, stop, tilt, forward-beak action, and repeat. Over and over, again and again. When one sandy patch has been thoroughly scoured, the ringed plovers relocate in sequence to an unploughed part of the beach.

Dot says farewell to the eider ducks and black guillemots who are now out at sea and who'll spend a large part of their day fishing before returning to their nesting sites along the river by the bridge.

This is a show we'll both come back and watch again. With or without the star turn, we give today's performance a standing ovation and Dot commits to memory the fleeting but fabulous highlight of her day. And like all the greatest shows on earth, this one was free of charge.

Living here, high in the Glens of Antrim, I am so lucky to see a wide range of birds that give me a real lift. Whether it's a pair of beautiful black ravens soaring above my yard making their very distinctive throaty croak, or a shy jay with its colourful plumage, or a rare sighting of a beautiful red kite, I feel blessed to be this close to our feathered friends.

LIZ WEIR MBE, STORYTELLER

© *Paul Hunter*

Ringed plovers (19cm) are members of the extended plover family. They have sandy-coloured upperparts, white underparts, two black bands across a white face, a black breast band and orange legs. They have a very short bill that is also orange with a black tip, and is perfect for foraging among shingle and sand in search of small shellfish, insects, and worms. They nest in hollow scrapes in the shingle and attempt to lure predators away by moving as if they are injured. Like all waders, male and female look alike.

Food and Water
Dot's Dos and Don'ts

There are a range of views on whether or not to provide food and water for birds all year round. Dot is of the opinion that if this is done responsibly then it can only be a good thing. She thinks it helps to split the year in two: March to September and September to March.

From March onwards, birds start breeding, the trees are blossoming, insects and flies are hatching. The great outdoors is slowly turning green again and places are coming back to life after the long winter. Birds are singing and different species are flying in from Southern Europe and Africa on a daily basis to breed in our woodlands and countryside.

This is the time of year that most of our garden birds pair up and either stay in the garden of their choice or move to hedgerows in parks, countryside and woodlands.

Blue tits, great tits, blackbirds, robins, dunnocks and house sparrows are more inclined to stay in gardens, especially if they have been able to source food there through the winter. They appreciate and become accustomed to the kindness of strangers. The ideal food for them and their tiny nestlings will always be live insects, like greenflies and spiders, found in bushes, ivy and trees. But they will have been well sustained through rain, hail, sleet and snow by feeders and fat balls in the colder months.

In summer, when the young fledge the nest, the parents will teach them what to eat, how and where to find food, the dangers they will experience and, in general, how to survive throughout the year, so that they can be self-sufficient.

It's important that feeders are maintained and cleaned regularly

to avoid the food going stale and potentially causing disease. In hot weather, clean water is very important, not only for drinking but also for bathing. Dot also believes that, like a lot of us, birds are fond of a good splash around in the bath. An old dish filled with water will provide birds with an enjoyable experience. When bathtime is over, on a fine day, the birds will sit in the sun, preening and spreading oil from their preen gland to help waterproof their feathers.

From around September, after breeding and feeding on the available food here, the migrating birds and their young will move back to warmer climates and to their old faithful food sources. Our young local birds must now get used to very cold and wet weather along with much shorter, darker days.

It's a shock to their system. The trees will soon be bare and insects have either died or are beginning to hibernate. This is the season when the birds will return to gardens that they've come to rely on for food and water, so it's important to wash and spruce up feeders and to check them for any damage.

As the weather deteriorates and winter draws in, more birds will depend on the food we supply. Black sunflower seeds, sunflower hearts, peanuts and un-netted fat balls are ideal. Blackbirds are very keen on sliced and diced apples and raisins.

Feeders, like bird tables, come in different shapes and sizes. A good plan is to start with one seed feeder. Mixed seed in small amounts will attract the birds. Keep an eye on it and if it disappears quickly then add more. The same principle applies all year round – if food is left and not eaten, it can go off and could cause infection, so discard it promptly. It's also vital to keep feeders as clean as possible.

Dot firmly believes in developing relationships with the birds and getting to know who's coming to the garden. Dunnocks, chaffinch, robins, house sparrows and thrushes will invariably be regular visitors. In winter, the tit families get together as a group, mounting a collective effort to find shelter and food. Long-tailed tits are especially amusing to watch as they hang upside down on fat balls in the feeder.

Fresh, clean water is critical throughout the winter months and making sure that bird baths or upcycled old dishes are spick and span is a daily chore. Dot's view is that if you have a cat, it's best not to feed the birds. Dogs and cats. Cats and birds. Never the twain shall meet.

Like all long-term relationships, it's important to keep working at it. Once you start feeding the birds, they will slowly but surely start to trust this kindness and begin to rely on it, so it's important not to stop. Dot has her own special winter garden coat in which she braves all weathers to fill the feeders and top up the bird baths. It reminds her as well that the birds don't have an extra coat to put on. All the more reason for us not to let them down.

Birdies, Eagles and Albatrosses

Obsessed by birds? No, my husband and I are not.
Doesn't everyone have two pairs of binoculars in the
kitchen? To watch what's happening in the garden,
even during meals? And everyone has another pair
upstairs because you can see more of the garden and
then there is the old spare pair in the car, just in case.
Totally normal!

JULIET FLEMING

Dot credits her dad with instilling in her a love and appreciation of birds and how they interact with each other and the environment. While she was honing her knowledge and skills in this regard around her childhood haunts on the County Down coast, I was at the opposite end of the country, in my home town of Portstewart, learning about entirely different types of birds on the north coast.

In the 1970s, a council-run summer scheme introduced me to golf and led to my lifetime fixation with the game. It would be many years later before I became curious and asked Dot if she knew why golf has a number of references to birds in its scoring system, such as birdies, eagles and albatrosses. Like me, Dot was puzzled.

At a certain age, it doesn't take much for a mind to retrace the footsteps of happy-go-lucky, youthful summers. In an instant, a wave of nostalgia transports me to one of my favourite places in the world: Tubber Patrick, the first hole on the Strand Course at Portstewart Golf Club. Named after the historic well on the Nuns' Walk nearby and from where St Patrick quenched his thirst, I think of this hole as 'the sleeping giant'.

As youngsters we called the Strand Course 'the big course'. In hindsight, that made perfect sense to nine- and ten-year-olds who played mostly on the 'wee course' at the other end of the town. With standard scratch scores of 64 for the boys and 67 for girls, this course was much more our size and a very good training ground from which to graduate to the imposing Strand Links.

Even then, in the mid-seventies, the ascent to the 1st tee at the Strand was followed by a moment of appreciation for the sheer breathtaking beauty of this unique golf hole. From the elevated tee, we towered above the summer holidaymakers on the beach below, tiny figures enjoying the soft, golden sand, sheltered by 6,000-year-old ancient dunes, cooled from the summer heat by a gentle breeze that carried their chatter and laughter to our unnoticed vantage point.

Let them swim and eat sandy sandwiches – we had golf to play. Four hundred yards, dog leg to the right, narrow fairway, tricky rough and a green the size of a well-manicured back garden. And just four shots to keep this sleeping giant at bay.

Portstewart's most famous and successful golfer, Maureen Madill,

Swan and cygnets at Portstewart Golf Club
© Portstewart Golf Club

has called this hole 'one of the best in the world'. Despite fluctuating character traits – one day a kindly friend you're glad to see, the next an intimidating stranger you'd rather avoid – playing this hole is as irresistible and unforgettable as an ice cream in Morelli's on the prom.

When the British Ladies Professional Open was played at Portstewart in 1982, I caddied for a South African player called Jo Smurthwaite. A keen 7 handicapper, I delighted that this accomplished international golfer placed such store by my local knowledge, and well remember her effortless birdies at this opening hole as she played each round of the competition. The farthest thing from my mind then was why this impressive score was called a birdie.

My reward for this job was a golf lesson for my least favourite shot – the fairway wood. Skilled golfers have an elegance that comes from natural talent and endless practice. Enthusiastic amateurs watch in awe and renew their vows to try harder. My fairway woods are less than elegant, but I never attempt the shot without thinking back to that generous lesson and the 4-wood-length cardboard box that arrived at the clubhouse two weeks after the tournament, containing a custom-made replica of Jo Smurthwaite's fairway wood with my name on it.

So it was with an enormous sense of pride and nostalgia that I found a place near that 1st tee on the big course in Portstewart on the opening day of the 2017 Irish Open to watch the best golfers in the world try to tame Tubber Patrick. And while the holidaymakers below carried on regardless, I took a moment to savour the beauty of this stunning place, grateful that my lifelong love affair with this great game began on a summer's day more than forty-five years before.

It would be a stretch to say that back then I noticed any other kinds of birds except for the golfing sort, but in recent years the irony of my birdwatching apprenticeship with Dot and my passion for this bird-referencing game is not lost on me.

It turns out that 'birdie' comes from the nineteenth-century American slang word 'bird', which was used to characterise something wonderful. The term birdie, which describes a score that is one under par for the hole, became common parlance in the 1910s. The exact origins of the term are unclear but one story goes that, in 1903, two brothers were playing golf at Atlantic City in New Jersey. One of them hit a second shot to a par-four hole that landed inches from the pin. His brother said, 'That was a bird of a shot'. He proceeded to hole the putt, giving him a score of three, one under the required target. There and then they decided that any future scores like this would be known as 'birdies'. The term stuck and before long travelled across the Atlantic and to golf courses around the world.

Given that the eagle is the American national symbol, it made sense to extend the use of bird references to define good scores and so the name of this most powerful bird was soon used to denote an even better score of two under par for a hole. Eagles and birdies are now fairly routine scores in professional golfing circles. But a three-under-par tally can be as rare as hens' teeth. Though, like a hole-in-one, it does happen. At this point, the British decided it was their turn to coin a phrase and, as an albatross is a seldom-seen bird, they settled on that title to describe this unusual achievement. A man called J.G. Ridland claims that he came up with the expression.

Joyce Wethered, a leading British woman golfer in the 1920s, suggested that a hole-in-one should be called a curlew or a whaup, an old Scottish name for this increasingly rare bird. It didn't catch on and to this day a hole-in-one is still known as just that. Perhaps Dot and I should start a campaign.

Condor, ostrich and turkey have also been used at times to describe various types of shots in golf, though none are in common usage today.

Despite never having played the game, Dot is a fan of golf courses and says that they are very good for a diverse range of wildlife in a mixture of ways. Grasses are laden with seeds that are a fundamental source of food to a multitude of insects. Parkland courses provide shelter for some nesting birds, and the naturally occurring flora and

The Strand Course, Portsewart Golf Club
© Airswing Media

fauna helps to balance the ecosystem, while also supplying food for bees, butterflies, moths and ladybirds. Links courses often feature sand dunes with long marram grass and thorny gorse and hawthorn bushes and can be a favourite nesting site for stonechats, meadow pipits and skylarks.

Each year, around April, warblers arriving from Africa are very glad of these ready-made nesting sites. Chiffchaff, willow warblers and grasshopper warblers will sing for a mate from the highest branch of any available trees, each trying to outdo their next-door neighbours. The female will then take time to decide which male is right for her.

Dot says that golfers on coastal courses should listen out for the singular call of the cuckoo in the spring as this bird delights in open spaces and therefore has a penchant for sand dunes. Kestrels and sparrowhawks will look for mice in any woodland that surrounds country golf courses, and robins, wrens, tits and thrushes will be found here too.

To the wonder of many golfers and the annoyance of others, in summertime, swallows may well be flying low around the greens, catching tiny flies. Dot worries that they'll get hit by a golf ball. In my case, even a birdie like that would be a long shot. In winter, waders enjoy the short grass of the fairways and the fringe around the greens as they can pick up worms or leatherjackets, and benefit from some shelter away from stormy seas and angry rivers.

My feeling is that someone with so much knowledge about birdies is bound to be a good golfer. The hope is that I can entice Dot to visit a golf course with a set of clubs, as well as her binoculars, at the ready, though I suspect that a round with her will focus entirely on birdies of the feathered variety.

Throughout my life, wildlife and nature have been my haven when I have struggled with my mental health. Nature is real, uplifting, a release from stress.

JIM, BANGOR

No Long Faces in Lurgan

*For years, blue tits have nested near the office window,
and what a pleasure it is to see the young birds thrive.
They often watch us through the glass, heads cocked
to one side, as if they're wondering what we're doing.
Perhaps they know that this 250-year-old library
carries the Greek inscription that is translated into
English as 'the healing place of the soul' and they
want to be inside too.*

CAROL CONLIN, ROBINSON LIBRARY, ARMAGH

A man once said to me, 'There's more to Armagh than Armagh.' And he was right. As the ecclesiastical capital of Ireland, the city is world-famous. It is a beautiful Georgian gem, largely because of Archbishop Robinson, a man sometimes described as 'the builder of Armagh' or 'the second founder of the city', and seen as a successor to St Patrick.

Archbishop Robinson was the architect of the Archbishop's Palace and the Stables. He restored St Patrick's Church of Ireland cathedral and installed the incredible organ that's still there today. He's also buried in the crypt there. Prior to his arrival in 1765, the Mall in Armagh was used for boxing matches and horse racing. But the Archbishop had other ideas and set about transforming it into a beautiful place to walk for the people of Armagh.

Carol Conlin has been the assistant keeper of the Archbishop's Library – the Armagh Robinson Library – for a number of years

Lurgan Park © Heather Geddis

and is an incomparable guide and expert on all things Armachian. In her tours she talks about the inscription in Greek above the door which means 'the healing place of the soul'. Unquestionably, this seat of learning exudes a tangible sense of calm.

Just up the hill and around the corner is No. 5 Vicars' Hill, originally built by Archbishop Robinson in 1772 as a Diocesan Registry and now a visitors' centre with an amazing range of early Christian artefacts. While there is much to marvel at here, the general consensus is that the archbishop considered his greatest achievement to be the Observatory, which he founded on one of the prominent hills around the city and which is still home to the oldest telescope in Ireland.

When you leave the city there's no need for a telescope to appreciate the apple blossoms that are truly resplendent in undulating fields alongside the county's roads and lanes in springtime. These roads lead to Richhill, Darkley, Camlough, Cullyhanna, Bessbrook, Keady, Poyntzpass, Laurelvale, Mullavilly, Derrymacash, Derrynoose, Dorsey,

Drumintee, Forkhill, Jonesborough, Newtownhamilton, Milford, and Maghery. To places with stories of their own to tell and with a shared, sometimes tragic, history, and to people with a strong sense of community and identity.

They say you never really know a place until you've walked in it. Or, in my case, until you've come a cropper in it. A short walk along the jetty at Maghery was the means by which I was supposed to board a small hand-crafted vessel for a trip on Lough Neagh to chat about the boatbuilding tradition in this area. Somehow, a gold ring I was wearing fell off and got stuck in the mud between the slats of the jetty. Thankfully, the local men I was with were not only skilled currach builders but also very handy with a crowbar and at removing slats on wooden jetties. The ring was rescued and my composure restored.

Navan is the sacred stronghold of Cú Chulainn, home of the famous Red Branch Knights and only a few miles from the city of Armagh. Coney Island is the lone island in the county. It's where Peter McClelland, the warden there for twenty years and a very smart man, once said to me, 'If you don't like your life, change it.' He spoke from experience and with the wisdom of a man who understands what contentment is. There are times when I can't remember what my telephone number is or where my car keys are, but I remember those words as if I heard them five minutes ago.

One of my greatest achievements in County Armagh was getting to the top of Slieve Gullion unaided and without the need for a rescue team to be dispatched. At 573 metres, it's the highest point in the county. The weather was cold and wet but south Armagh is a dramatic, rugged landscape that repays tenfold any effort to get to know it better.

The Ring of Gullion has a strong oral tradition and the people there are proud and honoured to pass on the knowledge and wisdom of their forebears to a variety of groups who visit, and to individuals in search of the real history of this cherished landscape. A woman called Una Walsh is one such custodian. She told me that the story of Brian Boru's funeral was handed down to her orally from her ancestors who were present at the religious ceremony. In these parts they say that if you kick a stone it'll tell you a story.

This particular day, Dot and I decide to pay a visit to Lurgan Park. The plan is that we'll kick a few stones in between meeting up with the birds from the county. I'll be surprised if Dot doesn't hear some great stories from her feathered friends as well.

Since the day and hour I heard the expression, 'a face as long as a Lurgan spade', I've wondered about it. So a rendezvous with Dot at the park in this market town seems like the perfect excuse to do a little digging with my own metaphorical shovel.

On the island of Ireland, Lurgan Park is only outranked in size and space by Phoenix Park in Dublin. It spreads out from an expansive lake and boasts 250 acres of walking paths, large green areas and a playpark. The centrepiece is a majestic, 59 acre man-made lake; literally made by men. It was dug by hand during the Famine as a means of creating work for the local people. After a hard, exhausting day's digging, it's quite possible that a worker's face resembled the long, heavy implement with which the backbreaking toil had been executed.

The park was once part of the Brownlow estate and is still overlooked by Brownlow House. In the mid-nineteenth century the lake was one of the largest hand-dug lakes in Ireland and also represented the flagship improvement to Lord Brownlow's demesne. It also contains the Coalbrookdale Fountain, a cast-iron structure originally erected in 1888 in Lurgan town centre to celebrate Queen Victoria's Jubilee. It's thought to be one of only four such fountains in the world and the last to still have its original lampposts.

Dot and I meet on Windsor Avenue at Brownlow House, also known as Brownlow Castle or Lurgan Castle, which dates back to 1833. As we go through the gates on this fresh, late-September morning, we imagine the grand life that the families who lived here must have known.

At any given time throughout the year, there is a plethora of birds to be seen and heard in the park, which makes it high on Dot's list of favourite places. Blackbird, song thrush, robin, chaffinch, house sparrow, blue tits and starlings are often around. In the summer, swallows, house martins and swifts are regular visitors. Jays make frequent appearances in the surrounding woodland and the lake is home to moorhens, coots, mute swans, great crested grebes, tufted ducks, black-headed gulls, grey herons and mallards.

Today, as we meander around the path near the lake, greylag geese are enjoying a light lunch of the verdant grass that's in plentiful supply. Dot explains the adults don't let the young out of their sights. Ever vigilant, they also keep a careful eye on any dogs that may be out for their regular exercise.

At peak times there can be up to two thousand daily visitors to the park, many of them dog walkers. Dot doesn't object as long as accompanying dogs are kept on a lead. She explains that the last thing the geese will want is for any pets or people to come between them and the water. If this does happen here, or at any similar outdoor space, the geese will feel very vulnerable and quickly make every effort to get to the safety of the water. Dot and the geese are eminently sensible beings.

Lurgan Park © Faith King

As well as coming to enjoy the green space, the playpark, and the supremely impressive, lime-tree-lined avenue, people also come to see the birds. In the lake, mute swans wait patiently along the water's edge to be fed by their admirers. The mallard ducks and greylags are there too but further out on the enormous pond, not quite as trusting as their good-looking cousins.

Accomplished birder that she is, Dot guides me deftly to what she calls 'her area'. She takes me to a spot by the lake where the reedbeds are more fringed, providing the dense cover that little grebes, moorhens and coots crave. She's been told that there is a kingfisher around but sadly there is no sign of this dazzling, colourful creature on the day we visit.

We make for the woodland path, where mature oak and sycamore trees stand shoulder to shoulder. The old brambles of ivy and hawthorn provide a five-star-quality home for wrens, robins, blackbirds and the entire extended tit family - blue tit, coal tit, great tit and long-tailed tit.

As we walk, Dot adopts a pose that tells me she's looking for signs of poo on the trees and I know she's searching for treecreepers. Like all good mothers, she says she doesn't have any favourites but I beg to differ and suspect that the treecreeper is her golden child. She says the white markings going upwards on the trees confirm that this is their territory and jokes that maybe they're having a meeting to divvy up the tree territory.

As we prepare to circle around the top of the lake, which continues to instil awe and wonder as we think of its construction, the habitat begins to change and varieties of long grasses become the dominant feature. The greylag geese and their families, in the company of the tufted ducks and gadwalls, prepare to say au revoir to their regular caller, while the black-headed and herring gulls are much more interested in what titbits might come their way. They might even be tempted to go fishing in the well-stocked lake for roach, bream or tench. Although they'd have competition from the anglers who can choose from a number of fishing stands peppered along the periphery of the watery basin.

On the way out, it's no surprise to hear from a passer-by that Lurgan Park was one of the first places in Northern Ireland to receive the prestigious Green Flag Award for providing a safe, secure setting that caters for the local community. Dot's also giving the park her seal of approval because it does exactly the same for our feathered friends.

Watching the birds flying and singing in my garden makes me feel closer to nature.

TINA McQUILLAN

© Ian Adamson

The **greylag goose** (76-89cm) is our largest resident goose. It is barred and mottled grey with white plumage, pink legs and a heavy, orange bill. Like all geese, it has a long neck, elongated legs. Male and female are identical. Greylags usually mate for life and, in an equitable arrangement, both parents share incubation duties and help with the rearing of their young. Baby geese move on to the water within hours of hatching. They're firm believers in safety in numbers and can be seen feeding in fields in large groups. Their motto might be, 'the more eyes watching for signs of danger the better'. At take-off, they create a noisy racket and fly in a V formation.

The Crows of Derrynoose

Working the early shift on BBC Radio and Television means a 4.30 a.m. alarm call, but then I get to hear the dawn chorus as the blackbirds, robins and wrens start to wake up too. The morning birdsong always puts a smile on my face and makes everything seem okay.

CECILIA DALY, METEOROLOGIST AND
BBC WEATHER PRESENTER

One of my favourite songs is 'Winds of Morning', written by Tommy Makem who is often referred to as The Bard of Armagh. A Keady man, he was a skilled musician, lyricist and a seasoned performer, highly regarded throughout the world for his immense musical talent. It seems to me that this song reflects Tommy's deep-rooted love of nature and the outdoors:

I've walked the hills when rain was falling
Rested by a wide oak tree
Heard a lark sing high at evening
Caught a moonbeam on the sea.

And in the chorus, he asks the winds to blow softly to guide him on his travels.

Peter Makem is Tommy's nephew and when I told him about my regard for his talented relative, he recounted this interesting story.

On regular visits back home for a holiday or a musical tour,

Navan Fort
© Navan Centre and Fort, Armagh

Tommy always made a point of visiting ancient sites like Navan Fort, Kilnasaggart, Newgrange or An Grianán of Aileach in Donegal. For some time, Peter suspected there was more to these regular pilgrimages than a search for spiritual solace and creative inspiration. And he was right. Tommy was in no doubt that two crows followed him when he made his way to these places. On his journeys to the top of Navan Fort, while meditating on how our ancestors ritually burned down their newly built temple, invariably two crows would make an appearance at the scene. The birds soared overhead and then landed on the adjacent trees, staring all the while as if transfixed by the reverential scene unfolding before them.

On one occasion, Peter went with Tommy to the standing stone on top of Mullyard Hill in Derrynoose in County Armagh, where Tommy duly performed the custom of putting his arms around the stone. Immediately afterwards, Peter noticed that Tommy was looking all around, skywards and along the bushes, scanning the landscape forensically. He quickly deduced that his uncle was waiting on and willing the crows to appear. This continued for maybe twenty minutes until, eventually, they began to walk very slowly back toward the car parked on the road, Tommy somewhat deflated as no crows had appeared.

Tommy stood at the open car door, delaying their departure, but there was still no sign of any crows. A shower of rain sealed the deal and the decision to move on was made. It seems the rain may have broken the spell and just as Peter turned the key in the ignition, Tommy shouted, 'Look! Look!' Straight ahead and coming in their direction was the familiar, deliberate rhythm of crows' wings in flight. No sooner had they appeared than they veered away to the left overhead in a great arc and were gone.

Peter recalls that his Uncle Tommy took all of this very seriously, though for a long time he remained at a bit of a loss when it came to an explanation as to why two crows seemed to appear on his mystical travels. That an abundance of crows in this country makes it probable that they will appear on a regular basis seemed a less than adequate explanation to him.

Tommy seemed to be in regular, intense thought about this unusual relationship with nature. Finally, he came to the conclusion that the appearance of the crows was entirely down to the fact that he was a singer with a deep interest in the song tradition, which in turn ultimately had its roots in the sounds of nature. After all, he had taken hundreds of age-old songs from his native county to the four corners of the world. He saw the crows as a sign of acknowledgement or thanks from nature, and maybe even as a gesture of solidarity. Those thoughts, Peter said, gave him intense satisfaction.

The final breakthrough in understanding came for Tommy when somebody asked him why it had to be a crow that appeared and not one of the more talented songbirds, like a blackbird, thrush or curlew? When he thought about it, the very expression 'a crow' was often applied in derogatory terms to someone who could not sing and hadn't a note in their head. In a moment of enlightenment, it all became crystal clear. The crow with its spikey squawk and grating sound was longing for the wholesome expression of its fellow singing birds. Tommy embodied this. Peter believes, as Tommy himself did, that Tommy was the human form of the great vocal affirmation of nature. This is why two crows invariably materialised when he visited the venerable sites of his native land.

Next time I'm in Keady or privileged to be standing on Mullyard Hill in Derrynoose, I'll wait for two crows to come into view. For fear of traumatising the birds, I'll quietly hum the beautiful tune to Tommy's prayerful song:

I've walked the hills when rain was falling
Rested by a wide oak tree
Heard a lark sing high at evening
Caught a moonbeam on the sea.

Softly blow, ye winds of morning
Sing ye winds your mournful sound
Blow ye from the earth's four corners
Guide this traveller where he's bound.

From 'Winds of Morning', song, words and music by Tommy Makem

*Birds have a huge presence in Celtic mythology. I live
and work in Armagh, which takes its name from the
Gaelic* Ard Mhacha, *meaning Macha's height. Macha
was a Celtic goddess, a supernatural being, a queen
– her name means a plain or a pasture and she is
associated with fertility, the produce of the earth, cattle,
dairying and horses. The Celts believed that Macha
would sometimes take on the figure of a raven or a crow
to caution people that death's door was near. She has
even been portrayed wearing a coat of feathers or with
a raven or crow hovering over her shoulder.*

DONNA FOX, TOUR GUIDE

WINTER

Robin © Alan Gallagher

Bangor Castle © Dot Blakely

Didn't We Have a Lovely Time the Day We Went to Bangor

Watching the seabirds wheeling in the sky along the coast has always been something I've loved to do. All the different gulls and terns, but especially the famous 'Bangor Penguins' – the black guillemots that nest every year between the rocks under Eisenhower Pier. They are such jolly little birds and the parents have been working flat out for weeks to feed their chicks and to teach their babies how to survive in a very big world. You can't not smile when you see a Bangor Penguin.

LINDA MCAULEY MBE

I didn't feel very inspired when Dot said, 'We should go the castle grounds in Bangor and look for poo.' Even when she added treecreeper into the sentence. But then again I know she has a sense of humour and loves nothing more than winding me up. Undeterred, I concluded that, either way, Bangor and the castle are always a treat to visit. Despite the weather behaving in an especially wet and windy way, I was buoyed up by the prospect of dandering round the tranquil castle grounds.

When the Ward family built their stately pile in the 1840s, naturally it wasn't open to the public. Designed in the Elizabethan–Jacobean style by Scottish architect William Burn, this elegant mansion has thirty-five bedrooms and a large, imposing salon, favoured at the time by the well-to-do for musical recitals. The site itself had first been occupied by Bangor Abbey – and its Franciscan friars – until the Dissolution of the Monasteries in 1542. At one point, the adjacent estate extended to almost 6,000 acres and included half of the entire town of Bangor.

The gardens are outstanding and have won many awards. There's also a museum to the Ward and Bingham families, which includes the Victoria Cross awarded to Commander The Hon. Edward Bingham, son of the 5th Lord Clanmorris. The last remaining member of the family, Lady Clanmorris, retained possession of the house until her own death in 1941. It is now the offices of the local council.

Dot knows this place like the back of her hand as Bangor is her home town. By the time I arrive, she has already put her 'bins' to good use in a surveillance operation.

After years of study, Dot is of the belief that if treecreepers think they are being watched as they prepare to scale a tree, they will just move around to the back of it and start the ascent from there, away from prying eyes. These aptly named birds are well used to people and, by and large, don't give them a second thought.

Mother Nature has kitted them out well to excel in their appointed profession – they have great, long toes that they use to dig into the bark and hang on with, three going forward and one at the back for extra grip. Treecreepers climb from the bottom of a tree. They have a stiff tail to give them balance as they get higher and circle the tree, picking up tiny grubs, spiders or ants as they go. Their bill is curved for easier access to gnarly parts of the tree bark. Dot says they are so well designed they can even climb and scrape out the soft husk of giant redwoods to roost in at night. At first light they will start feeding while they're on the move.

Treecreepers are small and well-camouflaged in tree-trunk colours and therefore can be hard to detect. Their call note is a shrill *tseee*.

Initially, it's tricky to hear and to distinguish it from that of other tree-loving birds. On this soggy day out, the strategy is to adopt the easiest method to find these clever little creatures. Dot's tried and tested approach is ... to follow the poo. The theory is that because they climb by hugging the tree trunk, everything else hugs it as well. These tiny birds are prolific in this department. As they scale the trunk, they leave behind a trail that the trained eye can spot pretty easily.

We approach a sizeable oak and follow the clues to the first branch and gaze upwards. If the treecreepers have ascended the entire length of a giant tree they are more than entitled to have a nap at the top to restore their strength. Not today though. The visible signs of their assault on the tree peter out and finally come to an abrupt halt. Dot says their modus operandi is usually not to hike to the top but rather to select a branch around the midway point, tiptoe along it, and then fly down to the bottom of the neighbouring tree to start all over again.

With pine, cedars, larch and ash trees in abundance here, the treecreepers have plenty of timber trails to choose from. In the course

Treecreeper poo © Dot Blakely

of their work, if the exertion proves too much, often they will find or make an indent in the bark to lean against and have forty winks. With considerably softer bark, redwoods are ideal for this and provide a very comfortable nap space.

Dot is at pains to point out that time spent birdwatching in the castle grounds will yield more than treecreepers. She has found nesting ravens in one of the gargantuan, ancient spruce trees that stand proud in an open parkland area well away from the castle itself. As is their usual practice, ravens call to each other constantly and fly high between the trees. Frequently, a nesting pair of sparrowhawks can also be heard. Dot has also been conducting a survey for the British Trust for Ornithology and can confirm that tiny goldcrests and roosting herons are also commonplace here.

Birds and beautiful old trees with enticing walking paths, not to mention a handy cafe in the nineteenth-century mansion, makes the mild soaking today well worth it. A good birding day out doesn't always have to be about perfect weather and good-looking, colourful birds. The talented treecreepers on the trees in Bangor Castle are testament to that.

© Alan Gallagher

Treecreepers (12–13cm) are mostly found in woodland and parks; they tend to avoid gardens, unless it's a very bad winter and food is scarce and they need to seek out nut feeders.

They have a white belly which hugs the tree bark. Their upperparts are mottled brown, providing good camouflage and making them hard to see until they start moving. They have three long toes pointing forward and one toe going back to cling onto the tree. They have a strong, long, brown, steely tail that works like a propeller as they hop around and around the trunk, all the time prodding into the tiny holes and cracks with their long down-curved bills, looking for spiders, ants and flies. They climb up the tree, scurry across a branch and then fly over to the bottom of the next tree to start all over again.

Their nests are made behind loose bark, large cracks or thick ivy, which is vitally important to a variety of miniature wildlife species. The best way to find these birds is to identify the tree they've been working on by looking for and then following the white poo trail they leave behind. This starts at the bottom of the trunk and circles upwards towards the top of the tree.

On my way back from an evening meeting, I looked up and saw nine swifts traversing the sky with acrobatic manoeuvres. The wonder of this sight had me smiling like a Cheshire cat.

Barry McKee

The Ravens of Scrabo Quarry

*The Dunavernary Flesh Hook was made by the
mystical Bronze Age metalworkers of north Antrim.
This beautiful artefact includes representations of
swans and ravens. Archaeologists tell us that the
swans are symbols of fecundity and the ravens are the
dark foreboding of death. But I like to think that our
ancient ancestors made it because they adored birds,
perhaps just as much as I do 2,500 years later.*

Keith Beattie, historian

At the top of Scrabo Hill, overlooking Strangford Lough and the
whole of north Down, is Scrabo Tower. Built in 1857, and 135 feet
tall, it's one of Northern Ireland's best-known landmarks, offering
spectacular views over the Ards Peninsula and Strangford Lough.

This large, pencil-shaped folly was built as a memorial to Charles
Vane, 3rd Marquess of Londonderry, and was originally known
as the Londonderry Monument. On journeys from Belfast to
Donaghadee, Millisle, Newtownards or Portaferry, I have glanced
admiringly at this intriguing structure, built on the site of a prehistoric
hill fort, and resolved many times to climb to the top. Like two larger-
than-life sentinels presiding over the town of Newtownards, both
the hill and the tower are worthy of closer inspection.

The name Scrabo also rewards further investigation. It is said it
derives from the Irish *screabach*, which means 'rough, stony land', and

which is also the name of the townland in which the hill is located. Dot has invited me to meet her at the cliffs at Scrabo Quarry. She says there are a variety of paths through the beech trees of Killynether Wood and around the disused quarries where you can catch sight of nesting peregrine falcons and ravens. Universal Pictures filmed several scenes of the film *Dracula Untold* in and around this location. Perhaps they needed some talented local extras.

Cursory research confirms that exposed quarry faces can still be seen in the South Quarry at Scrabo Tower. Since the mid-nineteenth century at least, the sandstone found here has been lauded as having 'an ornamental character'. Scrabo stone comes in a variety of colours, from warm, rich yellow, orange and deep red to paler grey and pink hues. Geological evidence shows that the variation in colour dates back to the eruption of the Antrim lavas sixty million years ago, when the hot, molten, magma caused changes to the paler, buff-coloured sandstone. Those lavas also created a sill of black dolerite that caps the sandstone, and this has protected it from weathering and erosion, and kept it well preserved. The high quality of the geological features in the South Quarry have afforded it exceptional status as an Area of Special Scientific Interest.

The sandstone at Scrabo has been quarried since at least Anglo-Norman times, the attraction being the variety of colours and the relative ease of working with this material. Scrabo sandstone was also found to be particularly suitable for intricate sculpture and carving work. One of the earliest examples of it being used in this way was for the ancient monastery at Greyabbey, where the oldest edifice dates back to the thirteenth century.

Scrabo sandstone was very much appreciated and sought after in the nineteenth century and was used to construct many buildings in the Belfast area, including Belfast Castle and All Souls Church on Elmwood Avenue. The development of the railways at this time made transportation of the stone much easier and led to something of a boom era for the industry.

Armed with my new-found knowledge of quarries and sandstone, and champing at the bit to witness birds of prey on these ancient stone cliffs, there was a definite spring in my step on the appointed early February morning. Dot has been watching peregrine falcons nesting in the quarry under Scrabo Tower for years. She says there's usually a fight in springtime between the peregrines and the ravens, who at one time lived in the lower quarry. Invariably, the peregrine is the victor.

Falcons are familial creatures and known to mate for life when they are in their natural habitat on isolated cliffs, far away from other pairs … and temptation. Dot recalls the winter that the Scrabo female peregrine got killed on the Comber Road. She says she remembers the male bird looking a bit frail and one of his wings beginning to droop. Days later he moved away and by the next spring, the cliffs had new tenants – Mr and Mrs Raven had seized the moment and moved around to the top quarry. Head of the household, Mr Raven was delirious with excitement, unable to hide his delight at the upmarket move and given to bouts of displaying: flying high in the sky, soaring and tumbling by turns in a dizzying demonstration of high-wire acrobatics. Raven males are jet-black, have big heads and eye-catching, diamond-shaped tails.

Mrs Raven was busying herself fixing up the old peregrine nest and calling patiently for her husband to lend a hand when he'd finished showing off to the neighbours. By the time of our visit, Dot was sure that the raven family were well settled and their eggs hatched.

There's a convenient Scrabo Tower car park beside the cliffs and Dot and I meet here, then walk up the steep hill, down past the picnic tables in the field and round to the well-worn grassy site and the best vantage point to see and hear the deep croaks of these captivating birds.

In no time at all, our hike is rewarded. Mrs Raven is out on patrol, looking up high and calling for her mate to bring back the dinner for their five hungry chicks, who already have their red gapes wide open in eager anticipation of the spoils of Dad's hunting. The devoted provider duly swoops in with an extra special treat for their young brood.

Ravens may not have eyes in the back of their heads but they have excellent vision and are very good at seizing the moment, skills which Dot surmised had been put to good use today as Mrs Raven begins the work of preparing a dead rabbit to feed the family. Ravens are, by nature, opportunists and Dot reckons that maybe this not-so-fleet-of-foot rabbit might have been injured or getting on a bit and not fit for the wily ways of the new raven on the block.

These birds don't have particularly sharp claws and are not overly strong as a rule, so they sometimes rely on other means to catch their prey. Their beaks do pack a punch, though, and they use them expertly to dismember mice, small birds, fish and insects with rapier-like speed. Just like some of the sequences in David Attenborough's remarkable films, scenes like this are hard to watch yet fascinating in equal measure. It is the circle of life in action.

Ravens have acquired a dubious reputation and in some quarters the collective name for them is 'an unkindness'. Dot says they are prone to fights among themselves, and more often than not this happens between members of the same sex.

We are mesmerised by the ravens. All of a sudden the big male flies towards us, turning at the last moment to send a quizzical look in our direction, as if to say, 'Have you never seen a family having lunch before?', and then taking up position on a nearby tree. We reckon he must have thought we were fairly harmless because he then gave a loud *crock*, which made the feathers on his crown and shaggy throat raise up, before he promptly flew back to his family. In the unlikely event that we get too close to the nest there is no doubt that he would attempt to intimidate us by lunging in our direction and cawing loudly.

Alongside the ravens, jackdaws also make their homes here.

Kestrel © Denis Chambers

Unlike their cousins the rooks, they don't sport feathery-style trousers on their legs and are much smaller than ravens. They favour the cracks and holes on the stony slopes of the deep quarry and band together in colonies, creating a loud din with their non-stop chattering. Operating at a safe, respectful distance, they remain wary of any approach by their larger neighbours and, in response, often lift in groups of up to twenty, flying in a circle before settling comfortably again.

A sighting of any bird of prey is particularly memorable. Since kestrels are extremely good at hovering, they are easier to spot than any other raptor. They eat small birds, lizards and large insects and from time to time they shop for dinner in and around Scrabo Quarry.

Occasionally they're spotted flying at lightning speed under the path where people are standing and hoping for a glimpse of this good-looking bird. With chestnut upperparts, black wing tips, and a grey-blue head and tail, the male cuts quite a dash. The females prefer to stay out of the limelight and can often be spotted sitting on a grassy ledge, hoping not to be noticed at all.

Kestrels are largely monogamous, and while a pair will separate over winter, they will come back together at the turn of the year when the male shows the female around potential sites, often in an area where they have nested before.

Along with blackbirds and a variety of tits, in summer the walk down to the bottom of the quarry will include sightings of willow warblers, chiffchaff, blackcap and white throat. The paths are steep, so caution and the right footwear is a must.

The robin, one of our most loved birds, is also very fond of this special place because of the natural shelter provided and the readily available feasts in the form of spiders, bugs and berries. Robins are, by nature, cheeky little birds and perhaps all the more charming for it. Their beautiful red breast marks them out as stylish and confident, never afraid to use their looks to their advantage.

Their call is an unmistakeable *tick, tick, tick,* and, without fail, this song will get louder with any encroachment on their territory, including from fellow robins. The male will sing triumphantly and forcefully to let his kinfolk know that he and his wife are settled here and visitors are not welcome.

© Jonny Andrews

Kestrels (34cm) belong to the falcon bird of prey family. They have long pointed wings, a protracted tail with a grey head, rump and rudder beneath chestnut wings with black tips. They are unique in that they hover. These birds of prey watch for the slightest movement in fields or grass verges then pounce instantly on unsuspecting prey. When the kestrel spots its prey, it drops vertically towards the ground at high speed, swooping to grab and stun with its bright yellow talons before killing with a swift bite. Kestrels can frequently be seen perched on top of telegraph poles and pylons to save them the bother of hovering.

As the female is usually at the nest site, she is well-camouflaged with chestnut and black feathers. Numbers of these beautiful raptors have been falling for some years due to the loss of traditional hedgerows alongside motorways and fields, meaning that food is harder to find.

© Stephen Maxwell

Peregrine falcons (38–48cm) are the fastest raptors in the world. Their prey can vary from their favoured pigeons, to large waders, geese, seagulls, and a variety of smaller birds, rodents and rabbits. Travelling at breathtaking speed, often from a height, ensures that a single blow from their large yellow talons will kill prey instantly.

They nest in quarries and on cliff ledges, where they have a good view of the coastline. They have a dark crown, white cheeks and are adept at stealing fish from other birds. They have hooded bills, dark eyes with yellow circles, a slate-grey body and wings that are broad and pointed for speed. The tail is short with light grey underparts. The peregrine falcon makes flying look easy and strikes fear in the heart of even the largest birds.

© Paul Hunter

Ravens (up to 64cm) are the largest members of the crow family. They are not as sociable as other crows and usually nest in sheltered cliffs, on rocky ledges and occasionally in large treetops. The raven flies higher than other crows, causing the large, shaggy feathers on its head and throat to stand out. The call is a loud *crock, crock, crock* and carries far. The body is all black, with a big head, broad wings, wide 'fingers' at the tips of their wings, and a diamond-shaped tail. Ravens stay in Northern Ireland throughout the year.

© Roy Crawford

Robins (14cm) have brown upperparts, and a distinctive red breast and face. The underparts have a pale grey-white border. Both sexes look alike, although the female can have a slightly more rounded belly. Robins are well known to gardeners as they often come close to get worms and insects from freshly dug ground and mown grass. With trial and error they can be coaxed to hand-feed. The males are vigorously aggressive in territorial disputes. Robins can be found almost anywhere, from hedgerows and thick shrubs in parks to woodlands and along coastal pathways.

Robins nest in thick ivy on trees, old tree roots, disused buildings, containers and undergrowth on banks. The female makes the nest using old leaves and small twigs to blend in with the habitat. Their brown upperparts give them good cover in the undergrowth while they are sitting on the nest. The male has a pleasant warbling song, made up of short phrases as he starts to sing. Dot maintains that very often he gets carried away and forgets the end of the tune.

Robins may be little birds but they make a huge impact when they appear. In Garrison I spend a lot of time walking in the park by the lake. This is where I go to escape from the pressures and strains of life. The robins follow me around and I find them extremely reassuring company. They have helped to inspire many paintings, especially at times when inspiration was hard to find.

MICHELLE DUFFY, ARTIST

An Enchanted Garden
in Antrim

The beauty, peace and tranquility of Antrim Castle Gardens provides welcome respite from the stresses of daily life and is a tonic for the soul. Watching the heron fish for his supper on the Six Mile Water river, listening to the song of the resident thrush or having a cheery hello from the robin provides pleasure and healing. The birds play such a vital role in soothing and lifting up our spirits in equal measure.

URSULA FAY, ANTRIM AND NEWTOWNABBEY
BOROUGH COUNCIL

A long, long time ago, I was an air hostess with British Midland and lived for a short time in Antrim just a few miles from the airport. So I have a soft spot for the town. Sadly, back in the 1980s, Antrim Castle Gardens on the shores of Lough Neagh bore no resemblance to the beautifully restored masterpiece it has now become.

In recent years, millions of pounds have been spent transforming this remarkable green space into something more along the lines of how it might have looked when Lord Massereene was in residence in the early part of the twentieth century. The remodelling is a triumph and the gardens are now rightly regarded as the jewel in the crown of Antrim and Newtownabbey Borough Council's public spaces.

Sir Hugh Clotworthy began building Antrim Castle in 1610 on

the banks of the Six Mile Water river and the gardens around it were laid out several decades later by Sir Hugh's son, Sir John Clotworthy. The distinctive Anglo-Dutch-style water gardens are one of only three in the United Kingdom, and the showpiece canals have also been meticulously returned to their former glory.

While the castle itself was extensively damaged by fire in 1922, Clotworthy House is still at the heart of the space and is open to the public. It was built around 1843 as part of the development of Her Ladyship's Pleasure Gardens. The building formed a stable block and coaching house to replace the castle's original coachyard, which in turn made way for the Pleasure Gardens. Alongside this oasis and the waterways, the gardens also include a twelfth-century motte and a parterre, an impressive ornamental arrangement of flower beds of different shapes and sizes.

Antrim and Newtownabbey Council, who are responsible for the gardens and their upkeep, call them 'a complex living museum containing over four centuries of culture and heritage that tell the stories of the people who created, lived and worked here.' The end result of the biggest garden restoration project ever seen in Northern Ireland is unique. No other outdoor space in Northern Ireland can compare with these four-hundred-year-old gardens. Ambition, determination, and sheer skill have created a breathtaking experience for visitors. And for that we should be truly grateful and immensely proud.

The prospect of both the gardens and the birds we will see there ensure that Dot and I arrive at the castle on the outskirts of the town in fine fettle. In neither respect are we disappointed. Dot hopes that we'll get to spend time with the thrush family, which includes redwing, fieldfare, song thrush, mistle thrush and blackbird. And, because of the many water features in this beautiful parkland, if we were lucky, we might just see a heron. This elegant, graceful bird is an unforgettable delight any day of the week and I am keeping my fingers crossed that today might just be the day.

On previous visits, Dot has also seen redwing and fieldfares here in the evergreen, ancient yew trees near the pond. They come here from Northern Europe between October and April to feast on the red berries found on our trees and in our hedgerows. You can also find them in fields feeding on worms.

From the car park, we head straight for the big trees in the idyllic walled garden of the castle, passing through the cafe courtyard on the way. Sadly, the trees have already been stripped of their berries and the birds have stolen a march on us and moved on. Dot is not a woman to be easily put off and, undismayed, we march through the arch to the woodland.

There are times when I think Dot has bionic, wonder-woman-strength hearing. Within seconds, her keen, all-natural antennae have picked up chaffinch, long-tailed tits, robins and blackbirds. What is getting her most excited though is a greenfinch, with its unmistakable *wizz, wizz* call. These olive-green birds also have a bright yellow wingbar and tail flashes. For a few moments Dot is in a trance as she revels in their distinctive song.

After we've had our fix of greenfinch, the 'find the thrush family' mission resumes, with fieldfare at the top of the list. This bird is quite big with a grey head and rump, chestnut back, black tail and spotted underparts. The redwing, on the other hand, is about the size of a blackbird, and has brown upperparts, a pale eyestripe, creamy, dark-speckled underparts and, in keeping with its name, red underwing parts. These birds can usually be found together, and with that in mind, we cross the little stone bridge to continue our search.

While the sun shines, sparkling and dancing on the water below, from nowhere there appears a beautiful heron, luxuriating in the glow of radiant winter sunshine and giving the impression he has little to do and all day to do it in. If these birds were people, we suspect that they'd be yoga teachers. They show every sign of having the patience of a saint and Dot assures me that they can sit for hours on end on riverbanks, waiting. Just waiting. Outwardly, without a care in the

Heron © Paul Hunter

world, but inwardly, on high alert, ready to pounce on passing fish or frogs that will be stabbed quickly and swallowed whole.

By and large they are solitary creatures. If they feel like a doze during the day, they carefully fold up their elegant necks and have a siesta. At night they sleep in the trees but nest collectively for added protection. Grey, black, and white in colour, a heron can be 90cm in height – that's three school rulers in old money. With supermodel-length legs, long, slim necks and sizeable, dagger-sharp bills for quick, precise fishing, it's no wonder they're sometimes called kings and queens of the river.

When herons walk, it's as if they are moving in slow motion: measured, thoughtful and graceful. Given their size, when they take flight, it's a different story; their huge wingspan makes it challenging to get in the air at all and, as they attempt to, they can look a bit clumsy and comical. Slowly, with necks drawn back and slow beats of their large, arched, black-tipped grey wings, they quietly fly away. Watching a heron is, in itself, a gift of tranquility and serenity.

Dot thinks herons are like creatures from prehistoric times. She has watched this wonderful large bird make its nest on top of a tall tree and settle itself entirely down into it for the night; an incredible feat of acrobatics, not to mention engineering.

Dot and I snap out of the stillness and head for the playing fields, where the fieldfares and redwings are having a keenly contested match that's all about who can find the most worms, while some nonchalant black-headed gulls look like they're acting as referees. We settle down to watch the game and I prepare to be wowed once again by Dot's effortless knowledge of the thrush family singers and their friends, the herons, keepers of the castle grounds.

Redwings (21cm) are about the size of a blackbird. Part of the thrush family, they come here in winter from Northern Europe. They can be found in trees and food-rich hawthorn bushes with their succulent red berries. Fields and playing grounds are also places where they hunt for worms,

© Paul Hunter

insects, and seeds. They have rich-brown upperparts and buff, spotted underparts; the red underwing can be easily spotted. They have a bold cream eyebrow and a broad, dark eyestripe. In flight, the red patches under the wing allow this little bird to leave quite an impression.

Fieldfares (25cm) are also members of the thrush family. They are slightly larger than redwings, though these two are birds of a feather, with similar culinary tastes, which means that fieldfares can also be found in trees and hedgerows that, at peak times, have an abundance

© Chris Henry

of crimson berries. Should there be a windfall of apples, both birds will be in their element. When fieldfares lift and head for the thermals, their call resembles a *chack, chack, chack* sound. They have a grey head, chestnut back, a grey and black tail and a spotted breast.

© Chris Henry

We have our own native **song thrushes** (23cm), as well as some that come to overwinter from Northern Europe. In spring, they can be found in woodlands and are very much part of our countryside song and are leading lights in the dawn chorus. They have a warble that can last for up to five minutes. It is loud and rich in tone with a succession of musical phrases. It comes in sets of three – the same three notes over and over, followed by a different note, repeated three more times. It's a blissful sound to hear at any time of the day. Classically handsome, this bird has brown upperparts, a white belly and a buff-coloured, spotted breast. Snails are its favourite food.

© Alan Gallagher

Mistle thrushes (27cm) are the largest of the thrush family. Our own mistle thrush is also a crucial member of the dawn chorus. Unlike other birds, they will sing in all weathers – in winter, its song is said to warn of an approaching storm, which is why it is sometimes referred to as the 'storm cock'. Their song is a prolonged series of short, flutey notes of varying pitches and they can emit a very powerful sound from the treetops, which the RSPB describes as 'similar to a football rattle'. They have grey-brown upperparts with a bold spotted grey-white breast.

© Paul Hunter

Our native **blackbirds** are also members of the thrush family. Some blackbirds also overwinter here from Northern Europe. The striking male birds are all black and stand at around 25cm. They have yellow eye-rings and bright orange, yellow bills. The females are dark brown with mottled, spotted undersides. The blackbird is one of the most popular dawn chorus songbirds. They sing in gardens, parks, and woodlands. The refrain is loud, full-throated with mellow phrases. In spring, there is no better way to start the day than at four o'clock in the morning, listening to their mellifluous contribution to the first-light singalong.

It's always a breathtaking moment seeing the old grey heron with his immense wingspan, his silent and hanging swoop, gliding into place on the edge of the bog. Still and patient, he bides his time … waiting for the right moment. There is much he can teach us.

ROSIE BELL, LACEMAKER

Rooks, Dippers and Clever Tails in Crawfordsburn

I love watching the buzzards and the flocks of yellowhammers that come to our farm to feast on the sunflowers and wildflowers over the winter months. It's just incredible. Sometimes we even spot barn owls with their distinctive call.

RICHARD KANE, FARMER

As a proud County Down woman, Dot is always keen to point out the attributes of the myriad places in her bailiwick that claim a special part of her heart. In a lifetime characterised by her love affair with birds, her fervour has taken her to familiar stomping grounds and to pastures new that have been a revelation and to which she returns time and time again.

Crawfordsburn Country Park falls into the former category. It's only two miles from Bangor and, more often than not, Dot walks there and back along the stunning coastal path that links the two places. In the summer months, the hay meadow that's part of the route is a blaze of colour with beautiful wildflowers luxuriating in the sunshine and swaying in the seaside breeze.

Helen's Bay is also close by, and its claim to fame is Grey Point Fort, which ranks as one of the best-preserved early twentieth-century coastal forts anywhere in the British Isles. It took three years to build and was completed in 1907. Two large guns commanded the entrance to Belfast Lough and were central in the defence of Belfast against naval attack. Sadly, in the Belfast Blitz of 1941, Grey Point was no match for the German air attacks on the city. In deference to this history, inside the fort today there remain two imposing twenty-three-foot-long guns.

As our visit is in February, Dot has guaranteed that there will be plenty of rooks. She says they nest in large colonies and love trees. They'll also be easy to spot at this time of year as the tall Crawfordsburn trees are looking a bit under-dressed, their bare branches not yet ready to develop new buds and shoots. Tall trees usually mean mature woodland and Crawfordsburn has this in abundance. Extensive tree planting on the estate, as it was then, really began in the eighteenth and nineteenth century when it was in the ownership of the Sharman-Crawford family. Scots pine, beech, sycamore and elm trees were favoured, while the glen was given a much more exotic feel with varieties like Monterey cypress, red cedar and Californian redwood. There are beech and laurel trees as well, and a dazzling array of rhododendrons. All in all, Crawfordsburn Country Park is a rooks' paradise, as the taller the tree the better they like it.

Dot hears the rooks before she sees them. To the untrained and potentially unappreciative ear this noise is nothing less than a racket. The sky above our heads is an avian version of what would represent a busy day for an air-traffic controller. The birds call incessantly to each other while on the move, flying in and out from their chosen tree, collecting what often looks like large, unwieldy and hard-to-carry twigs alongside smaller ones for the family home.

It's a treat to watch, though sore on the neck. But the strain is worth it as we witness these clever pilots follow precise flight paths towards small branches, which they snap off and then twist and turn until they are whittled to the required size needed for the repairs to last year's nest. It seems early for all this activity, but Dot says rooks are part of the crow family and breed early as a result of a diet of leatherjackets, worms and carrion.

A rookery © Juliet Fleming

As the numbers swell, the chatting and cutting of the twigs continues with intermittent fights about a particularly sought-after piece of nest-sized timber. Dot is in awe and wonder at the way bird's nests are all so different and made-to-measure for each species. Whereas I'm fascinated and impressed by what she tells me about the courtship rituals.

The male rook bows several times to the female he has in his sights. He drops his wings and, at the same time, caws and fans his tail. The female then crouches down, arches her back and quivers her wings, sometimes lowering her head and feathers while spreading her tail over her back. Often the male also presents the female with food in a final effort to impress her.

All of this has me marvelling at the amorous nature of rooks, birds that at times get the short end of the stick when it comes to image and behaviour. Sadly, my good opinion of them is dashed when Dot adds that often, after mating, nearby male rooks can attack the pair, causing the female to make a hasty retreat and perch in the safety of another tree. It seems there is more to rooks than meets the eye, but for now we leave them cawing in the Crawfordsburn trees and head to the river.

Dot has clearly called ahead to let the grey wagtails know that we are on our way. At the riverbank, there's a grand welcome in the form of a little group of these nifty movers standing on the stones in the water, wagging their tails and taking turns to jump up assuredly to catch tiny flies. Their flight is constant and deliberate along the surface of the river. The song is a *chipp, chipp, chipp* and the long, grey, streaky, flicking tail gives them the look and feel of mini flamenco dancers.

Grey wagtails sometimes nest under bridges or in stone walls near rivers. Blackbirds, chaffinches, robins and wrens are also keen on watery locations as it makes bathing, drinking and feeding on insects much easier. As we meander along the riverbank, Dot spies a comical little dipper settled contentedly on a rock to the side of the bank. She knows there is a breeding pair here but today he's on his own, and after some bobbing up and down, he disappears in an instant, flying upstream, leaving us wishing he hadn't been in such a hurry.

With so many ancient trees along the riverside, including giant redwoods and assorted pines, treecreepers are also in their element here. The unmistakable signs around the bottom of the tree trunks are proof positive: poo, poo and more poo. On previous visits, Dot has expertly tracked a treecreeper nesting site, which she says is in

Dipper © Alan Gallagher

an ideal location as people walk past and don't notice it. Precisely what the treecreepers want.

The park has a lot of different habitats and therefore a great variety of bird species: song and mistle thrushes, willow warblers and chiffchaff, blackcaps from South Africa, as well as local songbirds including chaffinch, robins and, of course, the inimitable, beautiful sparrowhawk, a full-time resident here.

This can be a quieter time of year as food is harder to find. In winter, some birds strike out for far-flung places in search of food and shelter. The warblers, including blackcap and whitethroat, will return to South Africa, but our local birds – robins, chaffinch, goldfinch and blackbirds – will be content to flit back and forth to their chosen gardens. Wrens usually stay in the woodlands in thick brambles.

Dot's usual habit is to walk up to the heart-stirring waterfall and then back down to the visitor centre for a relaxing lunch. As a rule, before she leaves she nips down to the shoreline to check on the gulls, cormorants, shags and oystercatchers, which can be seen on the rocks all year round. Eider ducks also breed on the coast here and can be seen with their young out at sea.

Today, though, we decide to take a last look at the wagtails before we head home. Animal behaviourists have long tried to work out the reasons that various species wag their tails. Cats sometimes do it when they're limbering up for a fight, and with dogs it's when they're happy and glad to see you. In the case of this gleeful, bantamweight bird, Dot and I opt for the romantic sentiments in this children's nursery rhyme:

And next there spoke the Willy Wagtail,
'I was once in love but I did prevail
I was once in love but I did prevail
And ever since, I wag my tail.'

Keep wagging, Mr Wagtail, keep on wagging.

© Juliet Fleming

Rooks (45cm) are members of the crow family, also known as corvids. They are large and bulky birds. The rook has bare, white skin at the base of its grey bill. The body is all black and they have feathers at the top of their legs, giving them the appearance of wearing shorts. They live in large social groups, nesting in tall trees and near farm buildings, flying together across fields, looking for leatherjackets and worms. They carry food back to the young in their throat pouches. They will all lift together in a noisy flight display, turning and twisting as they flash their diamond-shaped tails and broad wings.

© Paul Hunter

Grey wagtails (18cm) are elegant birds, usually found near water. With a long bobbing tail, they have grey upperparts with yellow underparts. The male has a black throat, white eyestripe, with grey upperparts and tinges of yellow below. Females are slightly duller and both sexes have black and yellow twitching tails. They nest in stone walls close to streams or fast-flowing rivers and feed by flying upwards to catch mayflies or small damselflies.

© Paul Hunter

Oystercatchers (43cm) are among the easiest waders to identify. They have black upperparts and white underparts, a red eye-ring, protracted strong orange bill and long pink legs. They are usually seen in large feeding flocks along the coastline and can open a muscle shell by stabbing it with their bill or hammering a hole in the shell. When the tide is high, oystercatchers, like other waders, can be found roosting on rocks or in fields feeding on worms.

Birds animate the garden in winter. When many plants have retreated below ground and the branches are bare, birds bring colour and life. A magical moment for me is when I hear the fluttering wings of a party of long-tailed tits arriving. I love how they always travel in groups – perhaps for safety, but I like to think they just love a good natter. Their badger-like faces are pretty, but what makes their visit special is its brevity. A quick snack on the sunflower hearts and they're off. Like the best performers, they always leave you wanting more.

DAVID MAXWELL,
Gardeners' Corner presenter, BBC Radio Ulster

Undercover in Wallace Park

Nature is a wonderful thing and a great stressbuster.

WILLIAM GUNNING, FARMER

———

For the twelve years that I lived in Lisburn, on most days I would go for a walk in Wallace Park. And I wasn't alone – it's such a beautiful green space it's not surprising that it's very well used by dog walkers, families, youngsters, cricketers and birdwatchers.

It encompasses 26 acres and was bequeathed to the town of Lisburn by Sir Richard Wallace in 1884 as 'a public park and recreation ground'. Initially it was called the People's Park but was renamed Wallace Park by the Town Commissioners after Sir Richard's death in 1890.

The layout of the park is still very close to the original design and retains a lot of its Victorian character, with the bandstand, duck pond and paths bounded by tall and imposing historic trees. The symmetry and inch-perfect lines of the Lisburn Cricket Club ground, which has its home here, are also impressive. The club is even older than the park itself, dating back to 1836, as is the duck pond, which was originally built in the seventeenth century as the town reservoir.

In 2010, Lisburn and Castlereagh City Council made a significant investment in refurbishing the park, including restoring the duck pond and bandstand and resurfacing the pathways. New lighting was installed, along with CCTV, litter bins and seating. A modern children's play area was also created and a new sports pavilion built beside the re-laid tennis courts.

Wallace Park really is a green oasis on the edge of the busy, bustling city that Lisburn has become. The Woodland Trust regard it as a particularly important site because it has many mature trees with deep roots, and the trees have lots of cracks and crevices in the bark for small birds to nest in and bats to roost on. The trees also provide shelter for the birds from the worst of the elements throughout the year and attract a wide range of invertebrates, such as caterpillars, aphids, moths, spiders and beetles, on which a variety of the birds who flock to the park will feed.

City parks like this one also play a crucial urban environmental role. Some trees are able to ingest toxic exhaust fumes produced by cars. They clean the air that we breathe and absorb noise from busy roads. More trees, more healthy people. As the meerkats would say, simples.

An area of well-manicured grassland is, in itself, a thing of great beauty but is doubly so when you consider that the lush grass also provides shelter for a range of worms, caterpillars and other invertebrates. These in turn are a source of much-needed food for the park's resident birds – rook, jackdaw, magpie, pied wagtail and robin. A small pond also attracts mallard and black-headed gulls, who visit to have a drink and a bath. At dusk, midges, moths and other flying insects will usually become active and they provide a rich source of food for foraging bats like the common pipistrelle and Leisler's bats. Biodiversity is alive and well and thriving in Wallace Park.

Dot had high hopes that on the day of our visit to the park we would find redwings and fieldfares – members of the thrush family who come here from Northern Europe to spend the winter. Neither of us had planned on the dark clouds that hovered threateningly over the park just as Dot drove through the entrance gates. It had been dull in Bangor when she set off and she was determined that the clouds would stay in County Down and that we'd dodge any looming showers. But sadly Dot's powers do not extend to the weather. On cue, the heavens opened as soon as she arrived at the park. Her wipers were working overtime as people ran for cover.

A minute later, I turned up, fully equipped with my giant golf umbrella; room enough for two definitely. No such thing as bad weather, just the wrong clothes or no umbrella. We are determined to find some birds and steadfastly splash our way through the puddles, heading for some shelter near the trees.

The birds are eminently more sensible – the redwings and fieldfares have flown to cover. We pass a few hardy black-headed gulls digging in the softened grass. Dot still isn't a fan but we agree to disagree. For this coastal girl, seagulls were the comforting soundtrack of my childhood. And they've got attitude, which I also like. I'm determined to convert Dot, but it's a work in progress.

Standing under a tree and the largest brolly in the world, the rain is pelting down and we are unusually quiet. Dot is straining to listen and determined that we'll hear or see something. She studies the tree we're under and explains how vital trees are, offering life-giving sustenance to the birds, ivy, spiders, flies and ants.

Suddenly, when we least expect it, the music starts to play. The wonderful song of the wren rises triumphantly above the splashing raindrops. He is resolute and ostensibly unperturbed by the inclement conditions. This is his place, his habitat, his kitchen. We revel in the *tick, tick, tick* while it lasts, which is not long – he sees us before we see him and scarpers into the thick ivy, a timely reminder of just how important this particular plant is for food and shelter. It may have been short-lived, but the song of the wren is beautiful enough to make the sun shine in anyone's heart, no matter what the weather is like.

Sitting in my garden one morning, I looked up at the fence and saw a sparrowhawk. Suddenly it snapped its gaze on me with a fierce look and then as quick as a flash, it was gone. I haven't seen it since, but sometimes I look at that spot and wonder.

SHIRIN MURPHY

© Alan Gallagher

Wrens (6–10cm) are found in woodlands, parks, gardens, countryside, at the coast, and in hedgerows. They're not our smallest bird – that's the goldcrest – but these tiny birds can make a very big noise. They vocalise a loud, explosive *tick, tick, tick* sound, followed by a long song. Very often you will hear a wren, but find it much harder to see one. Thick brambles, bushes or hedgerows are good places to start looking and listening.

This pocket-size bird has reddish-brown upperparts, grey-brown underparts and a distinctive white eyestripe. These features, along with a cocked-up tail and small pointed bill help with identification. Wrens feed on spiders, ants and flies from the undergrowth and tree bark. In the winter, they find it hard to find food, so maintaining hedgerows and brambles is especially important for feeding and shelter.

The other name for the wren is 'cave dweller', because of its ability to make circular nests with a tiny hole for an entrance – similar to a cave. When the cave, or caves, are built the male wren invites the female to choose one, and they become cave-mates. What she doesn't know is that this invitation may be made to several females in many caves.

A Right Royal Day Out in Hillsborough

I love to hear the healing soundscape of nature, birdsong of different tempos letting me know that all will be well. Each time I hear a cheery robin, it brings feelings of comfort and safety, and a beautiful spiritual reminder of my Granny Annie singing, 'When the red, red robin comes bob, bob, bobbin' along'!

ANN WARD, MEDITATION COACH

Many years ago I had a dog called Charlie. He was a very cute, black and brown Australian terrier who was bad with his nerves. The vet concluded that he may have been poorly treated early on in his young life. Through trial and error I discovered that the one place where he seemed to be at peace was in the car, which is he how he came to be my travelling companion on radio assignments that took me far and wide across Northern Ireland.

It turned out that this little canine soul had a spiritual side and he was particularly fond of Hillsborough Parish Church, just a few hundred yards from the main street of this village in County Down. Over the years, I'd been here a number of times to chat about this historic place of worship. Charlie and I would often arrive early and go for a dander around the impressive grounds, taking care not to walk on the beautifully manicured lawns on either side of the long path leading to the church. Botanists have confirmed that a number of the rarest species of wild flowers in the countryside adorn this sacred ground.

It was back in the twelfth century when St Malachy built his first church here, but there has been Christian worship in or around Hillsborough since AD600. Services on the site of the present church building date back to 1636.

The Hill family developed the now 'Royal' village of Hillsborough, and in 1663 Colonel Arthur Hill built a new church in the cruciform shape. The first Marquis of Downshire, Wills Hill, reconstructed the church in the mid-eighteenth century, creating the parish church as we now know it. Today it is a well-known landmark, not least because of its 180 foot spire, on top of which is a gilded cross.

Some of the plots in the graveyard also date back to the eighteenth century. Inside the church there are two magnificent organs, one designed by John Snetzler and the other crafted by his pupil, George Pike England. William Harty, whose son was the world-famous composer and conductor Sir Hamilton Harty, ranks among the organists who have played the illustrious pipes of St Malachy's. Sir Hamilton's ashes are buried at the west door of the church, near a birdbath designed by Holywood artist Rosamund Praeger and dedicated to him.

Dot has admired this picture-postcard church on her journeys through the village for walks around Hillsborough Forest Park. The park is only a few minutes from Hillsborough Castle, and with 150 acres to explore is a popular place for birdwatchers, walkers, photographers and nature lovers.

Some years ago, the park was redeveloped and now has upgraded pathways, lakeside viewpoints with seating, more picnic benches and car parking, and a state-of-the-art, woodland-themed outdoor play area.

The park's entire lake area is the showpiece of this environmental jewel, a forest temple for wildlife and home to a great variety of birds and animals, including foxes. The seventeenth-century Hillsborough

Fort can also be seen here. Built on the site of an old stronghold, the fort, which is square-shaped and features a parapet wall, was founded by Peter Hill in 1630. It was granted Royal Fort status by Charles II.

On our travels, my four-legged friend Charlie and I also used to walk around the huge, circular lake. Dot's only concern with dogs is that they are kept on the lead and away from any birds. Today she needn't worry about Charlie who has long since gone to doggy heaven.

After failing to spot them in Wallace Park, we're continuing our search for redwing and fieldfare, two of Dot's favourite winter birds. She says they have a penchant for the red berries found on hawthorn bushes and yew trees, and they can usually be found feeding in fields or grassy areas in public parks.

The first to welcome us when we arrive lakeside is a group of juvenile mute swans, showing off and acting boisterously in front of mallard ducks, greylag geese and black-headed gulls. The young swans are particularly impatient for the sumptuous repast they hope will come their way from their admiring fans. At the far side of the lake, cormorants sit with outspread wings, drying off after some precision diving. The tufted ducks don't come too close, but they seem to be able to feed themselves well enough by disappearing into the water and surfacing with beakfuls of waterweed.

As we continue to circumnavigate the woods, Dot hears and sees treecreepers, goldcrests, chaffinch, blackbirds and, as ever, brazen robins sitting on nearby branches, sure in the knowledge that they'll receive some tasty seeds from the budding ornithologists who recognise that time spent in Hillsborough Forest Park is birding bliss.

Across the bridge, Dot points to an area of reeds that makes good nesting for wildfowl and says good morning to some little grebe merrily feeding there. The search continues for fieldfare and redwing as we pass the parapet wall of the fort and pause to survey the large grassy patch, but they remain elusive.

Dot is disappointed. We resolve to come back another day. Maybe birdwatching is a bit like golf. No matter the quality of the golf, when

Swans at Hillsborough Lake
© Andrew Johnston

one round finishes, the next game is planned immediately. Then again, both pastimes can be surprising.

As we start the return journey and approach the final bridge near the entrance at the front of the lake, Dot stops suddenly to listen intently. A mistle thrush is offering an uplifting song by way of commiseration for his no-show relations. He's in no hurry to finish his performance and is blissfully unaware that a tiny high-pitched twittering call from a long-tailed tit is jockeying for position and Dot's attention.

Or maybe he is calling for his family to join him, because from a hedgerow, one by one, more and more long-tailed tits come into view. With more tail than body, they are aptly named. The adults continue chirping to the juveniles, issuing what Dot interprets as instructions to move to a new feeding site. Special moments like this enrich any bird walk. Just like finishing a round of golf with a birdie. All in all, very satisfying.

Long-tailed tits (14cm) have striking black, white and pinkish plumage. Their black tails are edged with white and are more than half the length again of their bodies. They have a tiny bill. The best time to see them is in winter when large groups come together, working as a group to find food.

© Gary Gray

They also roost tightly, cheek by jowl in cold weather. But in spring they strike out on their own and then pair up to build impressive oval-ball-shaped nests made from moss, lichen and spiderwebs. The nest is oversized to ensure that when all the young long-tails are inside, there is still space for the adults. Continually on the move and entertainingly turning upside down non-stop, they feed mostly on insects and spiders. In winter, they will seek out garden nut and fatball feeders and attach their small bodies and tails to feast on the fare provided.

Birds bring so much to our wellbeing, especially in winter when I put out my garden feeding stations, which attract the beautiful goldfinches with their red faces and gold wingbars. I often think they're more like exotic birds from warmer climates. Long-tailed tits also come with their families and the feeder becomes covered in tails. We are so lucky to have these birds on our doorstep.

Patricia Clark

Unusual Bird Behaviour

In the course of Dot's birding career, people have often sought her advice on an assortment of queries involving the behaviour of particular bird species. It seems that in the bird world, too, all life is here: from the surreal to the ridiculous, from the mundane to the phenomenal, from sad to tragic, and from quirky to downright comical. If Dot doesn't have an explanation, she makes it her mission to find one.

Magpie Wake

Despite their reputation as aggressive predators, there is a school of thought that, in fact, magpies have a warm-hearted side. Some animal behaviourists go so far as to say that these birds, in particular, feel grief and even hold funeral-type gatherings for their fallen friends. With this in mind, the story that two of Dot's students once told her certainly provides food for thought.

It was mid-March at around half six in the evening. From a bedroom window in their house in Holywood, County Down, two keen birders noticed a dead magpie in the garden, lying beside a large oak tree. Husband and wife both went to see if there were signs of any injury, but could see nothing and, in the meantime, decided to leave well enough alone.

At half past six the next morning, they were rudely awakened by the racket caused by a mischief of raspy, chattering magpies. Initial investigation through the window revealed one magpie standing beside their fallen friend. Before long, the bird realised it was being watched and quickly flew off to the nearby trees, where half a dozen other magpies were keeping watch on proceedings. As a group, they then also flew off.

A magpie wake © Cheryl and Jeremy Harbinson

Up and dressed now, Dot's students were intrigued and maintained a vigilant eye. An hour and a half later, a couple of magpies reappeared in the garden and started squawking and walking round the body. Once more, there were six to eight others perched in the trees above. It put the transfixed observers in mind of a wake. The birds, having again noticed the curious onlookers, flew away but returned five minutes later, by which point the fixated couple were camera-ready.

Two magpies walked around the lifeless bird cawing incessantly at it. One got very close and screeched loudly. After gently pecking at the body a few times as if trying to wake it up, the determined magpie finally moved around to the tail, picking it up in its beak and pulling at it. When that produced no reaction, it pecked harder at the body and head of the dead bird, squawking non-stop.

Then another bird walked over and tried a similar approach. When that also failed to produce a resurrection from the dead, the two birds slowly walked off across the grass and remained at a distance for several minutes. The whole thing was played out quite quickly, and during this time the eyewitnesses reported that the birds definitely seemed to be in a heightened state of anxiety.

At this point, a grey squirrel, who had been up in the oak tree probably wondering what was going on, scurried down the trunk of the tree and also walked over to the dead bird. It stood looking at it for a minute before losing interest, running off towards the garden bird feeder, where a bid to infiltrate this unattended food source was staged without success. By now, the two magpies had walked to the far side of the garden and shortly afterwards, perhaps having paid their respects, they flew off and didn't return.

The birdwatchers left the body for the rest of the day, but nothing else happened. They told Dot that they felt very fortunate to have been able to watch what they unequivocally believe was a magpie wake, right outside their bedroom window.

Dot is of the opinion that this is in fact what happened. She believes that many birds have the capacity to feel sad at the loss of one of their group or of a partner. She has heard of wakes for magpies before and of birds laying grass 'wreaths' beside the bodies of their dead companions, as well as of swans suffering distress if their mate is killed by another swan or predator. It's a heart-warming theory and one that may ensure new-found respect for magpies, often maligned yet highly intelligent creatures.

By Hook or By Rook

The collective noun for a group of rooks is a parliament. Over the years, Dot has also come across many stories about these birds and the significance, or not, of this descriptor. Rooks have been known to gather in a large circle around one or two of their fellow birds. People have reported seeing fights ensue and the birds in the middle being attacked or even murdered by the others.

A woman once told us that at a house in Sandholes in County Tyrone she was convinced she was about to witness violence of this sort perpetrated by a gathering of rooks. She was staying with her granny and while she was out in the garden, was stopped in her tracks by the sight of a large number of these highly social birds, circling one lone rook. Etched in her mind is the intimidating manner of the birds. Convinced that something dreadful was about to happen, she went back inside and hoped for the best. No dead rooks were discovered in the aftermath, so the jury on that particular day is still out.

On a lighter note, a man from Belfast with a house in Donegal told Dot a very edifying story about rooks playing in the wind. Some years ago, on a walk along Killahoey beach, from Dunfanaghy to Portnablagh, a group of birds were circling above the raised tee box on the golf course. It was a very windy day and the hole was about 20 feet above the beach. A diligent birder, the man knew right away that he was watching rooks in flight. But he felt there was more to it than just flying.

About fifteen rooks were taking turns to fly into the updraft created by the steep rise from the beach, and, as a result, were being tossed, almost tumbled, upwards. Working in ones and twos, it seemed to him that when they reached the top of the draft, they peeled off and re-joined the group at the bottom, as if they were taking turns to have another go. He watched in awe for twenty minutes and then had to leave. Backward glances confirmed that the rooks continued to frolic together happily. Rooks at play is his theory. He also says it was a magical experience and wanted us to thank the rooks on his behalf.

Dot believes that birds engage in fun and games with each other because they enjoy doing so. Rooks are very sociable birds and form very large flocks. They also initiate lifelong partnerships, called pair-bonds. The pairs then spend a lot of time together – feeding each other, displaying, vocalising and preening. Seasoned birdwatchers also report that the pair frequently act at the same time, copying each other's movements, so it isn't a huge leap of faith to imagine that they are partial to clowning around together too.

Dot was also told a story about a very well-mannered rook who became a regular visitor at a house in a rural area in County Down. The woman who lived there was well used to jackdaws visiting in the winter. They would arrive in noisy groups, hanging on to fatballs and gouging bits out of fat blocks. But one year, for two weeks in February, they were visited by 'Mr Rook', as they christened him.

He was always on his own and would wait patiently under the fatballs for bits to fall off before nibbling at them. Then he discovered the ground feeder cage with a fat block inside and learned how to poke his beak in and enjoy some of that too. He had a sunny disposition, and was always good-tempered and happy to wait his turn if the squirrel beat him to the cage for an early snack. If the lady went into the garden, he would fly off but only as far as the nearest tree, where he would sit and watch her. Little did this bird know how much enjoyment he provided as he plodded round the garden, every so often emitting a soft and gentle *caw*.

Angry Birds

The goldcrest is the UK's smallest bird. Despite its tiny stature, it's known as the 'king of the birds' and with its striking golden crest, this stunning bird usually makes quite an impact when it graces gardens with its presence. Unfortunately the two goldcrests that arrived in the garden of a house between Ballynahinch and Crossgar in the heart of drumlin territory did just that, but for all the wrong reasons.

This particular house is surrounded by a great deal of wildlife – otters, kingfishers, sparrowhawks, and bats. So when Mr and Mrs Goldcrest arrived, they were welcomed warmly, until it became apparent that their sole mission seemed to be to divebomb one of the downstairs windows, with their feet, wings or beak. Even pulling the curtains over seemed to annoy the angry birds and they squawked even more noisily. The intensity of the attacks gave serious cause for concern.

When Dot saw the photographs and video of the two birds in action, it didn't take her long to figure out what was going on. They were definitely angry, but also confused. The little goldcrest didn't realise that he was, in fact, looking at his own reflection. The male had his crest up to show the cheeky bird on the other side of the window that this was his territory and his female, and to make clear to the intruder that he was not welcome. The angrier he got, the angrier his imaginary enemy also became.

Dot says this kind of situation occurs pretty frequently. One solution is to put a large flower pot on the window sill. She has also heard of people using Windowlene or papering over the glass to discourage this behaviour and stop the birds getting sore heads.

Counting and Clicking
in County Down

*Sitting quietly by Strangford Lough watching the
wildlife go about their business, I am always reminded
that I am totally irrelevant to their activities. They
have no need for me. In that moment I am merely a
privileged spectator of the marvellous complexity
of their existence.*

RUTH MAXWELL

Dot has been a counter for the UK-based Wetland Bird Survey for
more than ten years. This is a monitoring scheme for overwintering
non-breeding birds and helps to provide data for the conservation of
their populations and wetlands habitats.

Since 1947, working under the auspices of the British Trust for
Ornithology, the skills and passion of birdwatching volunteers have
been used to advance our understanding and produce important
research that benefits both birds and people. So it's a natural fit for
Dot. She is also a major fan of the Royal Society for the Protection
of Birds and of the Wildfowl & Wetlands Trust. Each organisation
is quintessentially about conservation.

From September through to March, thousands of people
across the entire country take up positions along coastlines, lakes,
loughs and rivers, clickers at the ready, to begin the annual tally.
Dot's count zone is in County Down, from Anne's Point, along

Strangford Lough to Greyabbey.

The start time is precise: three hours before high tide. As the muddy or sandy shoreline starts to get wet, different waders with varying bill lengths move in sequence with the tide, feeding as they go, on tiny insects. As the tide washes over it, the much-sought-after eel grass, flattened by the mud, starts to straighten up and the brent geese, shelduck, wigeon and teal revel in the feast presented on this spectacular natural platter.

It is in this three-hour timeframe that the counters must keep tabs on the birds. Each volunteer knows their patch well. If Dot has a large group of brent geese feeding at Anne's Point, experience tells her that, before long, most of them will lift and move around to Greyabbey. It's vital that she follows them and relocates before completing her tally. She says it's a matter of having eyes not just in the back of your head, but on both sides as well. Passion and dedication are what keep Dot coming out in rain, hail, sleet and snow, year after year. To her mind, there is nothing as beautiful as a group of brent geese flying as a single body overhead, calling incessantly to each other.

Greyabbey is always worth a stop if you're in this neck of the woods. It's a striking little village on the eastern shores of Strangford Lough, half a dozen miles from Newtownards. The name comes from Grey Abbey, the Cistercian monastery founded by Affreca, daughter of the King of the Isles and wife of John de Courcy, the legendary Anglo-Norman conqueror of the province of Ulster.

The local people are known as 'Greba Cras', after Greyabbey and because of the large numbers of crows who live in the trees on the edge of the village. The same man who explained the provenance of this name to me also related a favourite yarn that locals have been known to regale visitors with.

In times gone by, when the abbey was inhabited by the monks and they wanted some feminine company, they would wrap their full-length habits around themselves, turn into crows, fly over the abbey wall, pounce on an unsuspecting woman and bring her back to the abbey, whereupon the magic would be reversed and the monks would become human again. When the monks and maidens were finished chatting and getting to know each other, perhaps over a fortified wine or two, the holy men used the same spell to become crows once again and fly the women back over the wall. As yet, neither Dot nor I have been able to confirm the validity of this anecdote.

Dot is often asked about the best time to see vast numbers of birds in and around Strangford Lough. Time and tide is the foolproof answer. As the tide begins to turn and recede, fully conscious that the water has done the hard work, the canny birds will arrive to feed on the wet mud. By the time the tide is in, the waders have now moved to one of the many islands in this huge expanse of water or to fields near the shoreline. Very sensibly, the geese and their many relations now sit out on the water, digesting their food and resting after their exertions.

With over one hundred islands, Strangford Lough can attract up to eighty thousand wildfowl and waders in the winter, making it one of the top twelve sites for seeing these birds in the United Kingdom. Whether you count or not, it's an open-air, free extravaganza well worth witnessing at least once in a lifetime.

The lough is a stretch of water that's full of interest: from the shipwrecked cargo liner *Empire Tana*, used in the Normandy landings during the Second World War and now easily seen from Ballyhenry Bay, to unusual free-floating knotted wrack seaweed and the aptly named Bird Island near Kircubbin that boasts the largest colony of cormorants in Northern Ireland. One visit to Strangford Lough is never enough.

Dot's gadget for counting is a small, pocket-sized, stainless steel contraption. It has four digits, which allows for counts of up to 9999 by using the tiny handle on the side of the machine.

In the same generous spirit that Dot has approached the considerable task of teaching her fervent birding apprentice, she's keen that I have a go with this clever hand-held device. Looking and clicking is easier said than done, so I start with the easy ones, which is how Dot refers to the swans, shelducks, mallards and the few eider ducks out on the water.

In fairness, simple arithmetic is usually my strong suit. For no particular reason, when I'm driving up and down and across the country, I add, subtract, multiply or divide the numbers on the car registration plates in front of me. If someone in the house needs a quick sum done they ask me, and the numbers bit of *Countdown* is my favourite part of the show.

But this type of numerical computation is well above my pay grade and I am happy to leave it to the expert for fear of any inaccurate reports of mightily increased or declining bird numbers in Strangford Lough. Satisfied with her reckoning, I stick to making tea, secure in the knowledge that Dot likes two cups, with zero sugar.

© *Paul Hunter*

Shelducks (60cm) have dark green heads, red bills, long white necks and a rust-coloured breast band across their mostly white bodies. They have a black stripe on their bellies, black wingbars and long red legs. Technically they are ducks but because these large wildfowl look more like geese, in some countries they're referred to as just that.

Geese have long necks and elongated legs. The male and female are identical and both parents help bring up the young. Ducks have shorter legs and necks and the males and females differ in looks. The males have brightly coloured feathers while the females have a much duller plumage that acts as good camouflage when they sit low on the nest in thick undergrowth. Males do not help to rear their young.

To have a tiny blue tit feed directly from my hand will live long in my memory. With my eyes averted I could see him eyeing up the seed and then he suddenly made that giant leap of faith and landed like a feather on my palm. Pure unbridled joy is the best way to describe it. I was overwhelmed that he trusted me so much to leave his place of safety and I felt really privileged. It was an amazing feeling – I really believe I made a unique connection with nature that day.

JIM RUTHERDALE

A Bird in the Hand
at Oxford Island

One day, when I was sitting in the back garden, a sparrowhawk landed on the roof of the shed. For a good five minutes he looked at me and I looked back at him. My guess was that he was thinking to himself, 'If only I could get half of his arm it would do me for a week.' When Val came out though the back door, he flew off but it was one of those special encounters that you don't forget.

RICHARD AND VAL WALSH

With a surface area of 151 square miles, Lough Neagh is the largest freshwater lake in the UK and Ireland. This vast wetland supports large numbers of wildfowl, including whooper swans, pochards, tufted ducks, scaups and goldeneyes.

It's an impressive outdoor space, internationally renowned and vitally important for birds. So, naturally, it's one of Dot's favourite places. Oxford Island National Nature Reserve sits on the south-eastern shores of the lough in County Armagh. As well as four miles of footpaths, five birdwatching hides, woodland, ponds, wildflower meadows, picnic and play areas, Dot says it's got a very good coffee shop and is a haven for people as well as wildlife.

Winding my way down the Annaloiste Road in the townland of

Oxford Island © Michael Graham

Derrytrasna on a cold December morning, I'm more than a little intrigued. Dot is being mysterious and says there's something special on the cards. She never disappoints and as we walk along a narrow path from the car park to the far side of the woodlands, soon we are not alone.

The gathering blue tits, robins and chaffinches seem to recognise their faithful friend and converge to greet her in a chorus of chirping that couldn't fail to charm the most cynical character. Dot says Oxford Island birds are very sociable and savvy, as visitors and locals have been feeding them in the winter, by hand, for years.

By hand. So that's it, by hand. Like a true bird whisperer, she says there's nothing to it. Dot puts some seed in the palm of her hand and edges closer to the hedgerow, all the while interpreting the contact calls emanating from the assembled mini masses. She looks away so as not to spook the bird. We stand very still, quietly. Soon, there's the sound of a faint tick close by and in the blink of an eye, something magical happens.

A second later Dot describes the feel of a delicate, tiny cold foot on her outstretched hand: the blue tit gently takes the seed and flies off to eat it in peace, away from a gawping woman with a microphone. I know what's coming. Dot and I switch places. I am tape-recorder free, frozen solid beside the hedgerow, seeded, hand outstretched, trying hard not to look.

'One is coming to your hand. Here he comes, here he comes. Wow, don't move,' whispers Dot.

I let the side down. Very badly. An involuntary, startled shriek on my part ensures that this particular tiny little bird will forever soar to dizzy heights to avoid this strange human being should there be any future encounters. But Dot's no quitter and, after some words of wisdom, she succeeds in securing another chance for me to prove to these innocent little birds that I, too, come in peace – and with seeds. Take two and a minor miracle happens. The bird lands on my trembling hand, gets the seed and disappears. I don't see it, I don't even feel it because the bird is so tiny and lightning fast, but I know I am in the presence of a unique moment that is good for the heart and soul of any living thing.

My unforgettable experience is just that. Dot assures me that I haven't been the same since. And for that, I am eternally grateful.

Blue tits (12cm) are popular little birds that can be found in many locations. They favour woodland, parks and, in particular, gardens. They have a blue crown, white cheeks, blue upperparts and yellow underparts, and like to hang upside down at bird feeders or look for caterpillars in the trees.

© Stephen Maxwell

They can fly into a variety of access holes in bird boxes and are the easiest bird to attract to your garden nest box. But don't be tempted to look inside. Like many species they may abandon the nest if they feel threatened. Remember it's against the law to disturb a nesting bird of any kind.

Every wild bird I see now is precious, every wild bird is sacred. To see any wild bird is to be connected, to belong and to find intimacy with who I am and where I need to be. They give us strength to carry on the only imaginable fight worth fighting for in the next days and years – to protect our wild spaces, our wild birds and ultimately ourselves.

JAMES ORR, FRIENDS OF THE EARTH

Acknowledgements

Firstly, thanks to Dot, not just for the experience we've had in writing this book but for many great days out together over two decades and counting. Her love for and knowledge of the incredible winged creatures that populate our skies, woodlands, rivers, parks and coastlines is a joy to be around. I can only aspire to her level of expertise, and after many years of patient tutoring, she continues to have my unfailing respect and admiration.

To Paula McIntyre for her love of birds, her encouragement and her sounding-board expertise, not to mention her many memorable packed lunches.

Thanks also go to my family – my mum Thelma and my dad Maurice, and my brothers Peter and Kieran. Special thanks to Dad for his poetry and occasional editing role and to Mum again for her necessary patience as a result and her weather forecasting skills. I am also thankful to many friends and cousins who were supportive from the first mention of this literary notion.

To all the generous people who contributed the short reflections that open and close the individual chapters, we can't thank you enough for the added dimension that your thoughts afford the book. Your respect and affection for birds shine through in each and every sentiment.

I owe a special debt of gratitude to the amazing people I have met in every county in the country over the last thirty years and who patiently introduced me not only to their place but to their birds as well. My interactions with all of you inspired many of the stories in this book. I am especially grateful to Patrick Cregg MBE, Sean Harpur, David and Olive Dunlop, Seamus Burns, Catherine Morgan,

Anne McMaster, Paul Clements, Liz Weir MBE, Keith Beattie, Selwyn Johnston and Catherine Scott.

To my colleagues at work, especially Michael Bradley (aka 'The Undertone'), and Ciara Johnston, who have provided unwavering backing for many of my flights of fancy, not least, my fascination with birds.

And to Jacky Hawkes, editor Patsy Horton and all at Blackstaff Press for making *Homebirds* happen after our many conversations about 'a book'. We should have known, Jacky – the clue was in your name.

ANNE MARIE MCALEESE

Thanks, of course, to my long-suffering husband, Terry; daughter, Tina; and son, Mark – they've had to listen to a lot of bird stories and facts over many years. Notwithstanding the fact that more often than not I would turn around to find that I'd been talking to myself, as they had all moved to another room. I might add, though, that in an innocent and touching act of loyalty, my grandsons Brandon and Ashton quickly came back in to listen to their gran.

Thanks also to my long-time friend Daphne who really gets the short end of the stick when we are out walking. She regularly loses me only to discover that I'm standing some distance away, binoculars fixed on something that has caught my attention.

A word of thanks as well to my wonderful friends, who, I'm blessed to say, are too many to be named and no doubt might be embarrassed if they were.

And to Anne Marie, my favourite trainee birder, for having the idea for this book in the first place. Now it's official – we are both homebirds.

And, finally, special thanks to Jacky Hawkes, Patsy Horton and all at Blackstaff Press for having faith in Anne Marie and me to put into words what birds mean to each of us.

DOT BLAKELY

The authors and publishers gratefully acknowledge the following individuals and organisations who generously agreed to the use of their photographs in this book:

Ian Adamson, Jonny Andrews, Albert Boyle, Denis Chambers, B. Cleary, Roy Crawford, Juliet Fleming, Pauline Gallagher (on behalf of the estate of Alan Gallagher), Heather Geddis, Terry Goldsmith, Michael Graham, Gary Gray, Cheryl and Jeremy Harbinson, Chris Henry, Paul Hunter, Andrew Johnston, Faith King, Stephen Maxwell, Aidan McCann, Paul McCullough, Brid O'Donovan.

Airswing Media, Ballyness Caravan Park, The Golden Eagle Trust, Navan Centre and Fort, Armagh, Portstewart Golf Club.

Index of Birds and Places

Entries in italic refer to photographs.